Praise for *Rebuilding Justice*

"Civil justice in America has serious problems, as Rebecca Love Kourlis and Dirk Olin vividly describe in *Rebuilding Justice*. This important book exposes unseemly judicial elections, the use of discovery as a weapon for extortion, and other distortions of justice. Kourlis and Olin also provide practical solutions that are certain to be influential in the inevitable battle to realign civil justice with the needs of a free society."

—Philip K. Howard, Wall Street lawyer and
best-selling author of *The Death of Common Sense*
and *The Collapse of the Common Good*

"This book couldn't have come at a more opportune moment. The American civil justice system is broken—jury service is in decline, the role of the judge has become bitterly politicized, the length and expense of civil litigation has made it prohibitive, and courts could not be less user-friendly if they tried. *Rebuilding Justice* offers a clear-eyed diagnosis of the breakdown of civil courts and jury trials and a lofty reminder of why our Constitution is alone in protecting access to them. This is a clarion call to repair the national treasure that is our civil courts system and a bracing lesson in what's at stake if we don't."

—Dahlia Lithwick, senior editor at *Slate*,
contributing editor at *Newsweek*, and former
guest columnist for the *New York Times*

"Court reform is the crucial third leg of judicial reform to go along with judicial election and recusal reform. As someone who has personal experience in a protracted and ongoing legal battle, it has become apparent to me that real judicial reform cannot be attained without all three. Whether you have been in court or not; whether you are a business person or a private citizen, the issues presented in this book should be of front-burner importance to you."

—Hugh Caperton, West Virginia businessman, plaintiff in *Caperton v. Massey Energy*

"This thought-provoking book should be required reading for all Americans. Our justice system is admired around the world, but, sadly, the state courts across this country are slowly failing. Change and resources are desperately needed. Unless we act and act soon, meaningful, timely, and affordable access to justice—the bedrock promise of the American constitutional experience—will cease to be real. We have no time to waste."

—John T. Broderick Jr., former chief justice of the New Hampshire Supreme Court and current dean of the University of New Hampshire School of Law

"This is an important book. It describes a crisis in our civil justice system that is not just brewing, but already fully brewed. And while others have written about many of these problems before, no one has drawn them together in so readable a form or sounded this clear and urgent a clarion call. Not everyone will agree with all the proposed solutions, but all are worth close consideration, and taken together they provide much food for thought—and action."

—Larry D. Kramer, dean, Stanford Law School

Rebuilding Justice

Rebuilding Justice

Civil Courts in Jeopardy and Why You Should Care

Rebecca Love Kourlis and Dirk Olin

Institute for the Advancement of the
American Legal System

FULCRUM

GOLDEN, COLORADO

Library of Congress Cataloging-in-Publication Data
Kourlis, Rebecca Love.
  Rebuilding justice : civil courts in jeopardy and why you should care
/ Rebecca Love Kourlis, Dirk Olin.
    p. cm.
  Includes bibliographical references and index.
  ISBN 978-1-55591-538-4 (pbk.)
  1. Justice, Administration of--United States. I. Olin, Dirk. II.
Title.
  KF8700.K68 2011
  347.73--dc23

                              2011029469

Printed on recycled paper in the United States of America
0 9 8 7 6 5 4 3 2 1

Design by Jack Lenzo
Cover image © Paul Kooi | iStockphoto

Fulcrum Publishing
4690 Table Mountain Dr., Ste. 100
Golden, CO 80403
800-992-2908 • 303-277-1623

www.fulcrumbooks.com

Table of Contents

Foreword

Our country's courts are in danger. Our democratic society depends upon the existence of a qualified and independent third branch of government. A healthy, fully functioning judiciary provides the counterbalance to the political branches that is necessary to assure protection of our constitutional rights. But support for judicial independence has faltered, in large part because our education system is failing to impart an understanding of the role and importance of the courts. We must rebuild public support for maintaining and protecting the courts.

This book is an effort to contribute to that project. I applaud its contribution to the general level of knowledge about the courts—for lawyers and nonlawyers alike. And I commend its observations about developing judicial selection systems that take cash out of the judicial selection process and that provide objective judicial evaluation tools to assure accountability.

We are blessed with many excellent judges and court staff around the country, in both the federal and state systems. But they and all the rest of us have an obligation to work hard to improve the system so that it is both impartial and accountable and so that it provides just and efficient resolution of cases. It is a duty that falls to all citizens, not just to judges and lawyers. This book should be of interest to individuals committed specifically to the health of the courts and, more broadly, to the health of our democratic system.

—former Supreme Court Justice
Sandra Day O'Connor

Preface

We gratefully acknowledge the invaluable assistance of Natalie Knowlton, research analyst with the Institute for the Advancement of the American Legal System (IAALS). Natalie helped us to synthesize our two voices into one; provided research and the benefit of her own work and knowledge on these various subjects; organized and checked our work; and generally made the train run on time. We thank you, Natalie. We offer our thanks as well to Jordan Singer, assistant professor of law at the New England School of Law, and Betsy Morris, former writer and editor with *Fortune* magazine and the *Wall Street Journal*. Jordy was involved in the early fashioning of this book and Betsy in the refashioning and reorganizing.

We further acknowledge those attorneys, judges, court administrators, and other participants in the system who lent their insights and voices to this effort.

Finally, we would like to thank the individuals, committees, and organizations with whom IAALS works. Without your input, support, constructive criticism, and creative optimism, this book—and the broader efforts to which IAALS is dedicated—would not be possible. Thank you.

Introduction

This book is an effort to sound the clarion call about the crisis in the courts in twenty-first-century America. Its purpose is to illuminate why courts are critical and how they are being eroded, defaced, and undermined—and to present some solutions, both internal and external. *Rebuilding Justice* is a joint product of two authors: one a former trial judge and state court justice who has seen the system from the inside for thirty years, and the other a legal affairs journalist who has made a career of following and commenting on the system from the outside. We hope that, between the two of us, we provide a balanced perspective.

Our stories differ, so we will begin them separately.

The Judge

After a few years in California, earning undergraduate and law degrees from Stanford University, I came back to Colorado and started practicing law. Over the following ten years, I practiced in a medium-size firm, a large national firm, and a Main Street law practice in a small agricultural town in Colorado. After that diverse experience, I became a state trial court judge in a small rural district in northwestern Colorado. I handled death penalty murder cases (my first being

two weeks after I took the bench, having never practiced criminal law), divorces, complex commercial
disputes, water cases, juvenile and probate cases. It
was a diverse docket in every sense of the word. I rode
circuit among three counties, over one very mountainous pass.

My first day as a judge, the docket was set in what
is referred to as a "cattle call" mode. In short, everything was set for two times: 9:00 AM or 1:00 PM. The
courtroom was packed. Prisoners from the jail were
seated in the jury box, with sheriff's deputies on either
side. Attorneys and their clients milled in the hall-
way and crowded the benches. It fell to me to call out
the cases in some numerical or other order. The long
and short of it was that everyone sat and waited while
other cases were being heard. The only person in the
courtroom who benefited from the docket method
was the judge. Everyone else waited, spent money on
attorneys, and wasted their time. That system was a
court-centric model—not a user-centric model.

After seven years on that trial court, I spent one
year as a mediator and arbitrator and then eleven years
as a justice on the Colorado Supreme Court. Over that
almost twenty-year period, I saw countless examples
of a system that is judge- and lawyer-centric, and not
citizen-centric. I found myself spending more and
more time advocating for the redesign of the system
and the reshaping of expectations—everything from
allowing jurors to take notes and ask questions of witnesses (written out, then passed to and posed by the
judge) to not keeping jurors waiting in a back room
while the judge and attorneys handle other matters;
from streamlining the way grievances against attorneys are addressed to sorting out the best way to

handle divorces for the benefit of kids and families. The citizens rely on the system, and they are the ones who should be at the center of it. It is my mission in life to work toward that goal.

It is also the reason I left the court to found and serve as the executive director of the Institute for the Advancement of the American Legal System (IAALS) at the University of Denver (http://legalinstitute .du.edu). The mission of IAALS is to identify problems within the legal system, research, propose solutions, support implementation of those solutions, and then measure their success. In short, we try to fix things that are amiss in the legal system in order to make it more responsive, transparent, efficient, and impartial. This book is the outgrowth and overview of that work.

I am not riding circuit as a trial judge anymore, but my experiences in that position shape everything I see and believe. I know how important it is for everyone who walks out of a courtroom to believe that they have been treated fairly.

My husband is a sheep and cattle rancher, and I often look to him as my lodestar. He has two maxims that apply here. First, if a system or a portion of a system does not make sense, something is wrong and needs to be fixed. Second, the measure of how much people care about something is how hard they are willing to work to make it better. There are parts of the legal system that just don't make sense, and I care about the system enough to work very hard at trying to change those parts.

The Journalist
I attended Dartmouth College on a debate scholarship, with every intention of going to law school. But my

passion for writing combined with a growing interest in politics to send me in a different direction—albeit one that eventually led back to the justice system. After graduating from Northwestern University's Medill School of Journalism, I covered Congress for the *New Republic* and the *St. Petersburg Times*. I met senators and presidents, dodged a bullet while writing stories about the Nicaraguan Civil War, and delved extensively into debates over Social Security and immigration. Occasionally, I also covered oral arguments before the US Supreme Court. That, along with research I conducted for a biography of William Brennan (written by Stephen Wermiel and published in 2010) increasingly led me into legal affairs.

In 1989, my wife and I moved from DC to San Francisco, where I took the helm of the *San Francisco Daily Journal*, a legal affairs newspaper, and eventually its sister glossy magazine, *California Lawyer*. Soon after our arrival came the Loma Prieta earthquake, and the newspaper's staff geared up in anticipation of a deluge of personal injury litigation. But it was the dog that barely barked. Relatively few suits were filed. During the ensuing decade, I developed a much more nuanced view of the civil justice system's failings and challenges.

Slip-and-fall lawsuits were not what were choking the docket, I concluded, but business-on-business litigation that was just veiled commercial strategy. Simultaneously, I became increasingly dismayed by the rise in private judging (via high-priced mediation and arbitration) and a growing politicization of the judiciary, with moneyed interests pouring dollars into a system that had once enjoyed a fairly broad expectation of nonpartisanship.

Toward the end of the '90s, I took a sabbatical,

studying immigration law as a fellow at the University of California–Berkeley's Institute of Governmental Studies. We then returned to the East Coast, where I launched what is today law.com and became national editor for the *American Lawyer* magazine. I subsequently collaborated on or directed many award-winning projects and features, including in-depth reporting on the fallout from the Enron scandal and the dot-com bubble bursts, as well as, most poignantly, writing on the liability fallout from the Catholic Church's child abuse scandals. I also wrote a column ("Crash Course") for the *New York Times Magazine* and occasionally contributed pieces on legal matters to the *Times'* op-ed page.

It was after writing one such piece—on the social corrosion I believed was wrought by New York's ferocious and secretive judicial election system—that I received backing to launch a think tank. The Institute for Judicial Studies inaugurated unprecedented journalistic tracking of a judiciary whose members were too often installed by shadowy backers and whose record of performance was so underreported as to be virtually opaque. We harvested metrics such as reversal rates, docket dispensation numbers, and motion practice statistics, with our work appearing in the *New York Times,* the *Wall Street Journal,* and *Newsweek.* When funding for that project ended, I became editor in chief of *Corporate Responsibility Magazine,* where my experiences are today serving a new readership.

Just as I was making that switch, Justice Kourlis approached me about working on this project, and I leapt at the chance. Justice Kourlis and the institute's reputation preceded them, and I eagerly joined as a fellow. My own writings about rebalancing judicial independence and accountability jibed with the IAALS agenda, and the opportunity to combine my reporter's pad with the institute's extensive research on civil justice reform has been well worth the nights and weekends that I sacrificed to the effort.

The Story

The justice system is fundamental to our democracy. The courts are the counterweight to the other two branches of government, assuring that no branch becomes overzealous. Our founders specifically established a system of government that is not pure majoritarian rule; rather, it is a system that focuses on protecting the rights of individuals—even against the majority if need be. The courts are the last line of defense for those rights—the safeguard. And, just to be clear, this is about more than the rights that attach to criminal prosecutions or defense. The legitimacy and trustworthiness of the courts underlie our willingness to enter into a contract, hire or be hired, buy a house, drive a car, or get married. The courts ensure that *all* of the rights guaranteed by the US Constitution and state constitutions are enforced and upheld. The individuals who wear the mantle of this responsibility include not just judges, but jurors as well. We are the only country in the world that has the benefit of a right to trial by jury in civil cases as well as criminal cases, and the enshrinement of that right in the Seventh Amendment was no accident. The courts were positioned to balance the excesses of the executive or legislative branches, and the jury to balance the excesses of the judges. Trial by jury—in all kinds of cases—was envisioned as an additional way to place power in the hands of the governed, as well as to ensure transparency and accountability of the court system. Lady Justice, more even than the Statue of Liberty, is the beacon of our freedom, our way of life, and our sustainability as a country.

Now, for the bad news.

Justice is in jeopardy, for a variety of reasons, but few Americans know or care. When the education or medical services systems are at risk, there is a national uproar. But, as chapter 1 addresses, because a majority of the American public does not understand the courts or recognize how vital they are to our body politic, there has been no public outcry about the justice system. (Speaking of understanding, for those of our readers who are not lawyers, you might find it useful to scan the Primer on page 193 and the glossary on page 224 before reading on. Lawyers whose practice does not regularly involve civil pretrial and trial practice might also find these sections to be a useful refresher course.)

One last introductory note: our focus is on court reform, not tort reform. Is that just a different consonant, a distinction without a difference, or perhaps just a less incendiary moniker for the same concept? No. Tort reform proposes amendments to the law that either limit the circumstances under which injured people may sue, limit how much money juries may award to injured people, or both. Court reform is a different animal. It is an effort to reform the *process*, not the substantive law. We believe that making the process work is the real objective: ensuring that if an individual or company has to file *or* defend a case, they will come away from the process believing that the judge was fair and impartial and that the process was just, efficient, and cost effective. That objective crosses all ideological and economic divides—it is a bid for a system with "justice for all." Court reform has universal application—and involves much higher stakes than tort reform.

Why is justice in jeopardy? We begin our exploration with some of the fundamental players who operate within these federal and state systems: the judges. Judges come to their positions in a variety of ways. At the federal level, the system is appointive—judges are nominated by the president, confirmed by the Senate, and then serve for life or until resignation, retirement, or impeachment. This appointment process is increasingly politicized and lengthy. Courts are often left with vacant seats for years while the president and the Senate alternately hold nominees hostage. In districts with heavy caseloads, dockets can languish. The battle over nominees in the Senate has trickled down to affect not only US Supreme Court nominees, but also lower court nominees, and party affiliation and doctrinal litmus tests can sometimes be predominate measures.

In state courts, where selection systems significantly diverge from that of the federal judiciary, these problems are heightened. Although something of a mishmash, those systems generally fall into three categories: appointment, election, or "merit selection." In states where judges are elected, judicial candidates—especially at the supreme court level—have run increasingly no-holds-barred expensive election campaigns in which they malign their opponents and align themselves with particular interest groups. One of the issues that judges and lawyers are debating in those states is how *much* money in campaign donations should cause a judge to be required to step down in a case involving a contributor to his or her campaign.

This presents sort of a *Price Is Right* question: how much does the perception of bias cost? On the other hand, appointment/retention systems are increasingly under fire as voters try to figure out what they should expect of judges and how to get the information they need in order to evaluate judicial candidates. In the meantime, even those retention elections are seen by some groups as an opportunity for making political hay, and judges are looking over their shoulders for fear of losing their jobs if they make an unpopular decision. On top of that, there is an entire movement that seeks to make courts *more* accountable to partisan ideology—a reasonable goal if judges are just one more species of political hack. But they're not, as we will explain in chapter 2.

Jurors are also fundamental players in the civil justice system, although they are rapidly vanishing from the courtroom. The Seventh Amendment to the US Constitution guarantees us trial by jury in most civil matters in federal court, and the state constitutions similarly provide for jury trials in many kinds of civil cases. We are the only nation in the world that guarantees that right. The jury is one of the ways by which our founders sought to protect against tyranny and ensure citizen participation in every aspect of our government. Yet, as we will detail in chapter 3, jury trials are now almost nonexistent in civil cases. Today, a tiny fraction of lawsuits filed actually go to trial by jury. Many readers might initially applaud that fact, thinking that juries are unpredictable, untrustworthy, and incapable of deciding today's complex issues. The McDonald's hot coffee verdict was big news for months, maybe even years. It was a 1994 product liability case in which a jury awarded $2.86 million to an older woman who suffered severe burns from spilled coffee she had purchased at McDonald's. The trial judge reduced the award to $640,000 before any appeal, and the parties then settled for an unknown amount under $600,000 before the appeal was concluded. Nevertheless, the case fanned a frenzy of concern about runaway juries.

The heat of that concern has since cooled, but jury trials have not rebounded. Before congratulating ourselves on stymieing that prospect, let us remember that the right to trial by jury was one of the fundamental tenets of the American Revolution. The Declaration of Independence listed "the denial of the benefits of trial by jury" as one of the offenses by England against the colonies. We fought for the right to have citizen participation in the justice system, to ensure that even the power of judges was not without limits or accountability. Let us also remember that jurors are us, and when presented with clear information and good instructions from the judge, we come to reasonable and trustworthy conclusions.

Jury trials have fallen prey not only to skepticism, but also to the expense of the pretrial process that depletes the resolve and resources of parties to a lawsuit before they ever get to a jury. The tortuous process of getting a case ready to go to trial (and paying for that preparation) might actually have the effect of ensuring that it never gets there. This is a trend we must reverse. When we as jurors are present in the courtroom, the whole process is more inclusive, transparent, and, well, democratic. It is the way the system was intended to operate.

Last, but not least, litigants are the fundamental users of the civil justice system. The faces of these players, too, are drastically changing. Particularly in state courts, but increasingly in federal courts, individuals are self-represented (in other words, they proceed without attorneys). The number of self-represented parties has increased dramatically in the last decade, either because people cannot afford a lawyer or do not trust lawyers, or because they do not think their case requires the services of a lawyer. The growing number of these litigants creates a unique challenge in the court system and plays into a number of the issues that will be raised in the chapters to come.

The shared component for these players is the stage on which they meet: the system itself. Our focus is the civil justice system—the taken-for-granted and much misunderstood civil justice system. Our Constitution and Bill of Rights, brilliant as they are, are not automated. They rely upon the courts for interpretation and enforcement. Think back in history to turning points in the American experience and the role of the courts. It was the courts that established the sanctity of contract (*Dartmouth College v. Woodward* in 1819); the protection of interstate commerce (*Wabash, St. Louis and Pacific Railroad Co. v. Illinois* in 1886); and the right to an equal vote (*Baker v. Carr* in 1962). It was in the courts where the agony of slavery played out and was finally addressed: holding first that a slave did not have the right to sue in court (*Dred Scott v. Sanford* in 1856); then that "separate but equal" facilities were constitutional (*Plessy v. Ferguson* in 1896); and finally that segregation was not permissible (*Brown v. Board of Education of Topeka* in 1954). It was the courts that ruled that unions and strikes were legal (*Commonwealth v. Hunt* in 1842) and courts that have parsed the meaning and application of the free exercise of religion clause (*Wisconsin v. Yoder* in 1972, holding that Amish children could be exempted from state school-attendance requirements). Courts protect personal property rights (*United States v. Causby* in 1946, holding that the government was required to compensate a farmer for his land when low-flying jets rendered it unusable); rights to free speech (applying protection of free speech to the states through the Fourteenth Amendment's due process clause in *Gitlow v. New York* in 1925); and free press (protecting all statements about public officials unless the speaker lied with the intent to defame in *New York Times v. Sullivan* in 1964). These were all civil cases. Civil courts are the byways for the establishment of norms and the enforcement of rights and remedies.

Our nation's history is marked by times when the courts were both the last resort and the vision for the future—breathing life into statutes, holding people accountable, and providing "Equal Justice Under Law." The role of the courts in our brand of government is to enforce the rights constitutionally guaranteed to individuals—against even the will of the majority. All of us are members of some minority with rights that we hold dear. Without the courts, those rights could be quickly eroded. However, the impartial, efficient administration of justice is imploding, and a number of factors are to blame.

At both the state and federal level there is a complex support structure for the courts. The on-the-ground manifestation of that support is clerks, jury commissioners, and administrators who run the courthouses and undergird the judges. More broadly, both the federal and state court systems have administrative offices that supervise budgets, train judges and staff, develop plans and analyze implementation, and maintain information systems. This complex support structure is at risk as courts face free-falling budgets.

Legislators are urging the courts to figure out ways to cut out case types, cut back services, reduce jury trials, and add more folks who act as judges (but who are really not judges) to resolve cases more cheaply. In another corridor of the legislature, lawmakers are mandating that certain kinds of cases be expedited or given priority on the docket. Criminal, juvenile, and family cases necessarily move to the front of the line, and civil cases languish at the back. This is a multi-faceted problem that, as we will discuss in chapter 4, threatens to destroy the system from within.

Into this mix comes the fact that the rules of civil procedure guiding federal courts and many state courts were crafted in 1938 and have not been fundamentally revised since then. A great deal has happened since 1938; enough to make it feel like ancient history. With population growth, changing demographics, and the advent of the digital age, the playing field is larger and more complex. Compounding the issue are the judges and lawyers who are change-averse and trained to spell out every possible contingency. The result is complexity, and with complexity comes delay and skyrocketing cost. The rule of thumb among lawyers around the country today is that a lawsuit must involve at least $100,000 to be cost-effective. So if someone defaulted on your $50,000 promissory note, for example, you might not be able to find a lawyer to bring the case. It is no wonder, then, that more and more litigants are proceeding through the court system without being represented by an attorney. We will explore the interplay of the rules of civil procedure and the issue of costs in chapter 5.

The cost of litigation is one of the factors driving this implosion of the civil justice system. *Litigation* is the formal name for the lawsuit business—and it *is* a business. In this business, discovery is the name of the game, not trial. Discovery is the process by which the parties to the lawsuit demand information from each other. That information can come in the form of written questions, inspection of documents, or oral examination under oath. Discovery can be used and abused not to seek truth, but rather to increase costs, cause delay, and create inconvenience—all with a view toward leveraging settlement. Plaintiffs routinely complain that defendants stonewall them and manipulate them to ensure that the costs go up so that they will take less for their case. Defendants complain that plaintiffs hold them hostage by filing thin cases, demanding broad and deep discovery, and leveraging settlement possibilities.

Take document discovery as an example. In 1938—and indeed up until about 1988—it was not unusual for a lawyer to show up in court for a trial with one or two files of documents. That same type of case can now generate thousands or even millions of documents that need to be reviewed and perhaps produced to the other side, including e-mails, text messages, voice mails, and multiple drafts of documents. Under the current rules, *all* of that information can be mandatorily discoverable even if it has only a tangential connection to the case. The costs of electronic discovery in a medium-size case can be in the millions of dollars. Chapter 6 will explore the consequences of data overload to the functioning of the civil justice system.

The problems of court funding and excessive

litigation costs can come together to reduce access to both the state and federal civil justice systems for all but the very wealthy. This is, however, not a death knell—provided that there is the necessary support for innovation and solutions, as we will explore in chapter 7.

Finally, the issues identified above—budget crises, expensive and time-consuming pretrial procedures, and reduced access to courts—are even more acutely felt in family cases, where the very nature of the process involves litigants in crisis. Chapter 8 will explore the issues faced by children, families, and individuals as they move through the domestic relations process.

So walk with us through the courts of the second decade of the twenty-first century as we chronicle the problems and identify some possible solutions. This is important stuff; the courts require the support of a knowledgeable and attentive citizenry if they are to continue to guard the ramparts of our way of life.

1
Civics and the Courts: A Crisis Hidden in Plain View

Most Americans do not understand the courts, and what we do not understand we will not prioritize, much less fix. We are at risk of losing something critical to our democracy, in part because too few of us comprehend it and value it. This is truly ominous for a branch of government that lives or dies by the faith and goodwill of the American people. Without that faith and goodwill, the courts lose their legitimacy and judges become robes with no authority.

Unfortunately, what we cannot see as a society, we are not likely to understand—and we see less and less of what happens in courts. Root causes of the new opacity include the vanishing jury trial, the rise of resolution of disputes through private arbitration or mediation methods, and a litigant preference for sealed settlement agreements. While these trends do offer some possible benefits (in that they can reduce the cost of resolving a case and also decongest the courts), they also combine with the loss of court beat reporters and contraction in traditional media coverage to obscure and distort the public's view of the system.

If justice is not perceived as being served, perhaps it is not served at all. Participants or observers of specific litigation can come to the belief, rightly or wrongly, that justice has not been served. More broadly, the citizenry can become cynical—deriding jackpot justice when they find outcomes random, or special interest justice when they suspect the system has been gamed. Only the most sensational civil cases make the news (with the exception of the blogs), and they are likely not representative of the millions of cases that flow in and out of courts every year. This might explain much of the reason for the increasing attacks on the civil justice system. Insurance companies and businesses fear that juries find liability too easily and dole out excessive damages. Individual litigants think injury compensation takes too long, is oppressively expensive, and is a David-versus-Goliath proposition in any event. Others fear that civil litigation has become a piggybank for powerful lawyers who monetize technicalities and churn cases.

Arriving at a consensus about these varied claims is somewhere between extremely difficult and impossible, in part due to the lack of objective data and the fog that surrounds the courts. Without data, partisan interests can too easily hijack reform initiatives. Greater transparency and dissemination of that data would help the public and policymakers alike improve their understanding of the system, assess its performance, and soberly evaluate reform alternatives. The judiciary itself, with assistance from a more publicly communicative bar, must take the lead in opening the courthouse windows and switching on brighter courthouse lights.

That is no easy task. The ignorance about the system is pervasive and horrifying. For example, the chief justice of one state recently reported that after his presentation to the legislature on budget requests for that state's courts for the upcoming year, one member of the budget committee approached him and noted that he had never really understood that the judiciary is a separate and equal branch of government, rather than just another executive administrative agency. And although Senator Chuck Schumer (D-NY) who serves on the Senate Judiciary Committee surely misspoke when he listed the three branches of government as the House, the Senate and the president,[1] this omission is symptomatic of the backseat role our third branch of government all too often occupies in the public's perception.

The black hole of misunderstanding is dangerous to the health of our body politic. Surveys sponsored by the Philadelphia-based National Constitution Center (NCC) conducted in the late 1990s reached profoundly depressing conclusions about Americans' civics knowledge, generally, and their legal knowledge, specifically. In the first comprehensive study of constitutional knowledge, the NCC 1997 survey found that one in three surveyed did not know the number of branches in the federal government.[2] Of those surveyed, 62 percent could not name all three branches, only 14 percent could name one, and a mere 15 percent could name two.[3] In a 1998 poll, the NCC found that more American teenagers (59 percent to 41 percent) could name the Three Stooges than the three branches of government.[4] Even worse, 94.7 percent could identify actor Will Smith, but only 2.2 percent could name the chief justice of the United States.[5] (Okay, we like Will Smith, but *really*?)

Speaking about this later study, former mayor Edward Rendell, who subsequently became governor of Pennsylvania, explained that this was not some abstract, neoconservative lament about the decline of

Western civilization. The implications, he said, were much more concrete than that. Rendell crystallized the impact of this reality in words that are still sadly true. "These results are alarming for everyone who cares about the future of our democracy," he said.[6] "The Constitution doesn't work by itself. It depends on active, informed citizens. And that's who these kids are: our future citizens."[7]

Rendell's assertion was subsequently borne out in a plain and practical study published by Professor Kimberlianne Podlas in a 2002 issue of the *American Journal of Trial Advocacy*.[8] Using the coinage "syndi-courts" to describe the syndicated judge shows on television, Podlas reported how watching such programs affects the opinions of prospective jurors.

Podlas's conclusion was that these shows have created a unified body of misinformation. Easily digestible narrative lines of legal conflict are glibly wrapped up and resolved. As such, the shows capture nothing of the complexity that informs the liberty or property tussles in real-world courtrooms. Or, as Podlas nicely distilled it: "These shows rely on aggressive, often unsympathetic judges, laughable litigants, and simplistic legal results."[9]

Podlas demonstrated that the syndi-court programs (*Judge Judy*, *People's Court*, *Divorce Court*, and the like), filling the vacuum of some citizens' civics knowledge, can have significantly damaging effects. When viewers have no actual knowledge of the system, the syndi-courts' mischaracterizations take root and grow malformed expectations.

The study encompassed 225 individuals reporting for jury duty in Manhattan; Washington, DC; and Hackensack, New Jersey. Group members were asked whether—and, if so, how often—they watched any of the syndi-court shows then being aired. Of the 225, almost two-thirds (149) were frequent viewers (checking "two to five times per week" on number of times watched), and 76 were infrequent ("once per week") or nonviewers.[10] Some might find the fact that two-thirds of the individuals plunked themselves down in front of a syndi-court show two to five times per week disturbing enough in its own right.

The consequences of "television law school" are positively jaw-dropping. The findings here, as described by Podlas, were hardly subtle. Apparently having internalized a televised judicial role model that prizes snark, cant, quip, and put-down, frequent syndi-court watchers viewed judges as active participants in the dispute. They expected the judges to have an opinion and to make this opinion clear to the jury. They expected them to ask questions, be aggressive with litigants, and express displeasure or disbelief.

The significance? Those viewers expect judges to be participatory, partial, invested decision makers—not independent and impartial arbiters. As adduced in a seminal piece by Judge Bruce M. Selya for the *New England Law Review*, the justice system's skeletal structure might consist of rules and principles, but its lifeblood is the collective respect derived from public opinion.[11] When a majority of the public obtains its central understanding of law from television—and when that programming is dominated by legal soap operas and courtroom game shows—fundamental misperceptions of the system's purposes and processes are like a virus invading a compromised immune system.

Granted, these findings might be dated. Surely, a decade of Internet access must have elevated the national awareness on this front? Well, no. A 2007 Annenberg Public Policy Center Judicial Survey found that only one in seven Americans surveyed (15 percent) can correctly name John Roberts as the chief justice of the United States.[12] But two-thirds of those surveyed (66 percent) knew *at least* one of the judges on *American Idol.*[13] In a 2008 study of American adults by the Intercollegiate Studies Institute (ISI), more than twice as many respondents (56 percent) knew that Paula Abdul was a judge on *American Idol* than knew that the phrase "government of the people, by the people, for the people" was a quotation from Abraham Lincoln's Gettysburg Address (21 percent).[14]

Most observers believe that American civics illiteracy is acute, chronic, and epidemic. Of the more than two thousand people to whom ISI posed its nearly three dozen questions, fully 71 percent received a failing mark.[15] Importantly, the plague is trans-demographic. ISI chairman Josiah Bunting III noted that the failure cut across all segments of the population. "Young Americans failed, but so did the elderly," he reported to the National Press Club in 2008.[16]

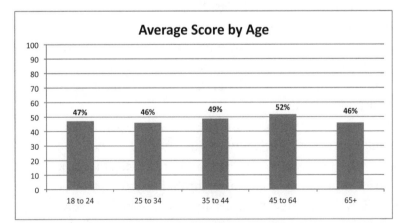

Our Fading Heritage: Americans Fail a Basic Test on Their History and Institutions (Intercollegiate Studies Institute 2008).

It does not end there. Bunting reported that "men and women, rich and poor, liberals and conservatives, Republican and Democratic, white, black, yellow and brown—all were united in their inability to master the basic features of America's constitutional form of government."[17] The overall average score was 49 percent—an F in any classroom.[18] Nor could partisans of any particular faction claim bragging rights. Liberals scored 49 percent, conservatives scored 48 percent, and independents and Republicans scored only slightly higher than Democrats (52 to 45 percent).[19]

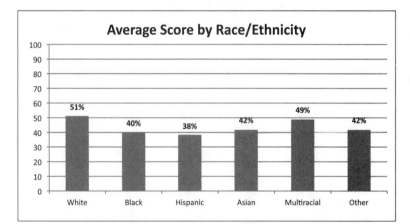

Our Fading Heritage: Americans Fail a Basic Test on Their History and Institutions (Intercollegiate Studies Institute 2008).

Some apologists for the status quo respond that this is why we depend on representative democracy to develop expertise, or at least working knowledge, among those chosen to lead. Again, the news is not good. As indicated by that legislator's ignorance of the governmental branches, politicians might not get it either: they scored more than five points *lower* than their unelected cohorts.[20] The number of officeholders who knew about the establishment clause was 21 percent.[21]

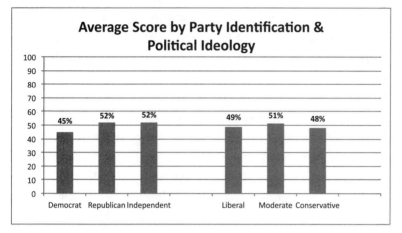

Our Fading Heritage: Americans Fail a Basic Test on Their History and Institutions (Intercollegiate Studies Institute 2008).

Our Fading Heritage: Americans Fail a Basic Test on Their History and Institutions (Intercollegiate Studies Institute 2008).

Others argue that education is the Holy Grail. If so, the current chalice is filled with Kool-Aid. College graduates did outscore those who didn't get a college degree, but not by as much as one might hope (just 57 percent to 44 percent).[22] "For each year of college attained,

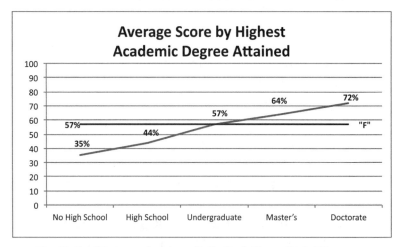

Our Fading Heritage: Americans Fail a Basic Test on Their History and Institutions (Intercollegiate Studies Institute 2008).

college graduates answered only one more question correctly than their high school counterparts," ISI's Bunting said.[23] "If you can get as much civic education from a library card and newspaper subscription as you can from an expensive college education, then something is terribly wrong with the activities on our campuses."[24]

If children are our future, as Governor Rendell asserted, and the health of our Constitution and judicial system rests on education, then we have much to fear. A 2009 survey of Arizona high school students attending public, private, and charter schools confirmed the grim reality of the previous surveys.[25] The survey pulled from the US Citizenship and Immigration Services database of questions given to citizenship candidates. The passing rate was 3.5 percent for public school students, 7.3 percent for charter school students, and 13.8 percent for private school students.[26] In comparison, Citizenship and Immigration Services reported that candidates for US citizenship, who are required to take a test on ten questions from the database, had a first-try passing rate of 92.4 percent.[27] Even acknowledging that the candidates for citizenship actually studied these materials for their test, shouldn't there be a corollary requirement for native-born students?

The combination of misinformation, misconception, and syndi-court-shaped perceptions is toxic. And most courts are not themselves trying to change the brew by infusing the mixture with real information about the functioning of the courts and their role in our democracy.

To be sure, at least one significant critique has been made of the consensus on civic ignorance—by professors James L. Gibson of Washington University in St. Louis and Gregory A. Caldeira of Ohio State University. In "Knowing the Supreme Court? A Reconsideration of Public Ignorance of the High Court," the pair denigrates "open-ended recall questions" that they claim do not reveal the true extent of the citizenry's knowledge of the Supreme Court.[28] Instantly recollecting the chief justice's name, they contend, is not as important as general ability to locate the purposes and powers that reside within the governmental structure. Gibson and Caldeira claim that "people know orders of magnitude more about their Supreme Court than most other studies have documented."[29]

Even if one concedes that this study is not an outlier (which it might well be), it is focused on the Supreme Court per se. It does not undermine broadly demonstrated public misunderstandings of judicial independence and the impartiality of the courts in general.

Take this construction that is partly based on Gibson's research:

> I do not know the name of my plumber. But when
> the plumbing gets stopped up, I know how to

get a plumber to come out and repair my plumb-
ing. I may not know at any given moment who is
most responsible for the detention camp at Guan-
tanamo Bay. But when I hear discussion of this
issue during the election season, I likely learn who
is responsible (even if I might soon forget); and,
perhaps more important, I learn which political
party, not individual actor, is responsible.[30]

Political parties depend upon some level of Americans' knowledge of their system, but Americans' choice
of judges and funding of the courts need to be as independent as possible of constituencies. There is a vital
difference between homeowners subcontracting pipe
repair and citizens who farm out their informed participation in participatory democracy. An uninformed
citizenry leaves more than water damage in its wake.

Moreover, in the end, even Gibson grants the
enormous and unique importance of public knowledge in this realm:

> Politicians and scholars worldwide have long been
> impressed with the fragility of judicial power.
> When it comes to securing compliance with their
> decisions, courts are said to have neither the power
> of the "purse"—the ability to raise and expropriate
> money to encourage compliance—nor the power
> of the "sword"—the ability to coerce compliance.
> In the absence of these tools, courts really have
> only a single form of political capital: legitimacy.
> Compliance with court decisions is contingent
> upon judicial institutions being considered legiti-
> mate. Legitimacy is a normative concept, basically
> meaning that an institution is acting appropriately

and correctly within its mandate. Generally
speaking, a great deal of social science research
has shown that people obey law more out of a felt
normative compunction deriving from legitimacy
than from instrumental calculations of the costs
and benefits of compliance.[31]

There is no army standing at the ready to enforce
court orders. Indeed, the rule of law is a bit like our
monetary system—built on trust. But trust is easily
eroded and must be constantly earned.

Thus, the dearth of understanding about the courts
can itself put our system at risk. Even Gibson makes
the case for heightened awareness (i.e., knowledge) to
preserve the "reservoir of goodwill" that is required to
protect a minoritarian bulwark:

> If democracy can be simply defined as "majority
> rule, with institutionalized respect for the rights
> of the minority, especially rights allowing the
> minority to compete for political power," then the
> judiciary clearly represents the "minority rights"
> half of the equation. If courts are dependent
> upon majority approval for their decisions to be
> accepted, then one of the most important political
> functions of courts is in jeopardy.[32]

The point is that courts should not be *dependent*
upon or look to the will of the majority when enforcing rights; and if the majority does not know that, the
courts are in jeopardy of being not just misunderstood
and maligned but, more ominously, hijacked by partisan
interests. The necessary complexity of our nuanced civil
justice system—and the unique vantage point occupied

by members of the bench—makes the judiciary itself the first, best Paul Revere in this cause. Among those who decry the almost viral ignorance of our court system's true role, retired justice David Souter is one who believes that such ignorance has become so threatening that he has volunteered to wage a high-visibility public campaign to combat the disease.

Citing another poll that had just found two-thirds of the country unable to name the three branches of government, the normally reserved Justice Souter became apoplectic. "Consider the danger to judicial independence when people have no conception of how the judiciary fits within the constitutional scheme," he said.[33] "If anyone put that question to my ninth-grade class...none of us would have failed to answer."[34]

Retired justice Sandra Day O'Connor has embraced this cause as part of her life's work as well. Justice Souter's voice, in fact, was echoing that of his former colleague. In 2009, calling the rift between citizens and their legal system "positively frightening," Justice O'Connor launched an education campaign, including a school-targeted website called iCivics.org. She told the National Education Association:

> For a good many years, I think public schools, by and large, were conscientious and tried to teach civics and government. We have some very boring textbooks on the subject. Certainly most of them weren't written to keep you awake. Nonetheless, we persisted...[But] in recent years, Congress and our then-President proposed federal money be given to school districts based on test scores in math and science, on the theory that schools doing a good job in those areas should be rewarded with some

funding. The unintended result was that many
schools stopped teaching civics and government.[35]

Justice O'Connor proceeds from the same assumption as former Philadelphia governor Rendell that
representative democracy is organic in nature and
thus dependent upon an active, informed citizenry. In
Justice O'Connor's case, the twinned notions of do-
it-yourself government and rugged communitarian-
ism took root on the Arizona ranch of her childhood.
"You can't avoid participating in the productive life of a
ranch or farm," she told the *Arizona Republic*.[36] "It takes
everybody's help to make it work. You learn how to be
part of it and how to do things. When you live out a
life like that, you can't look up in the Yellow Pages and
get a repairman if something breaks. You have to fix
it. You."[37] (Those who would suggest that all of us just
have to know how to call the plumber, take note.)

Hardly a member of the Nintendo generation,
O'Connor nevertheless recognized the implications
of a population whose children spend an estimated
forty hours per week in front of electronic screens
(whether TV, computer, or cellular). Looking to har-
ness that reality, her iCivics initiative includes plat-
forms for Web-based games designed to teach seventh and eighth graders about government. In one,
for example, a middle school student sues his school
for banning a T-shirt he wears that features his favor-
ite band. It's a real-world primer in First Amendment
issues that relates directly to teen experience.

But the former justices' laudable efforts must be the
floor, not the ceiling. Or, as Jon Stewart commented
when Justice O'Connor revealed the public ignorance
statistics on *The Daily Show*: "We're going to need more

than a website."[38] For one thing, it is sadly ironic that the iCivics games—in which players can watch and listen to a Supreme Court argument—offer greater access to the courts than real life affords. What Judge Richard Posner has dubbed the law's "professional mystification" is an anachronism that both shrouds the law in secrecy and diminishes the collective democratic character. The administrative governing body of the federal courts recently announced a pilot program to test the feasibility of allowing camera coverage of civil proceedings in federal district courts—much more appropriate for our edification than syndi-court programs. Moreover, beyond the curricular shifts wrought by No Child Left Behind reforms, docket management that discourages trials and media coverage that deemphasizes court cases have also helped decimate public understanding of the courts in recent years.

We have also lost jurors as a pool of informed citizens. For years, jury service was not only a significant way for citizens to have a voice in the system but also a way to learn about it. In the twenty-first century, however, jury service is virtually extinct in the civil realm.

Given these trends, it is increasingly falling to judges themselves to communicate their message to the broader public. This marks a change from the courts' traditional role of communicating primarily through activity in the courtroom or written opinions. In fact, many judges remain squeamish about any public outreach—except from behind the bench or the pen.

Take this question: should judges be blogging? Although former federal judge Nancy Gertner was an occasional blogger for Slate.com, one of the judges on the First Circuit Court of Appeals—the same Judge Selya who championed the public confidence as the lifeblood of the legal system—has voiced fears that such practices could come back to haunt judges if any comment is deemed prejudicial to a subsequent case. Indeed, when a judge ventures forth to educate or inform the public (from whatever platform or podium), there is the danger that he or she will say something that will boomerang and show up in a motion to remove (recuse) the judge from a case.[39] The very reason that judges avoided those public venues in the past was because of a concern that they would slip over into statements that could be used to impugn their impartiality.

That might be a luxury judges no longer have. A hypothetical future cause for recusal should not become the enemy of the much more urgent need to promote legal literacy. The danger is now not the stray motion to recuse, but rather the ubiquitous misunderstanding of what courts do and why they do it.

Both at the level of educating adults and at the level of venturing into classrooms, there are examples of just that kind of outreach. In Colorado, the Our Courts program provides nonpartisan information programs to adult audiences to further public understanding of the state and federal courts in Colorado.[40] A judge or a judge/lawyer team, with the benefit of visual aids and handouts, conducts an interactive discussion to explain how the courts work and also presents on the process and procedures of different case types. These public education efforts are no longer optional. Anything short of that consigns us to a longer residency in the legal dark ages. Judges must go on the road, or the Internet highway, and take the lead in telling the story of the courts.

In short, for us to fix the courts, we must first understand them.

2
Gambling on Judges

At the very heart of our system is the judge—the keeper of the constitutional flame. How do we choose and monitor those judges? What do we expect of them?

Justice Sandra Day O'Connor carries a copy of the Constitution in her purse. She refers to it when the subject of judicial selection comes up and reminds her listeners that the framers created a nonelected judiciary in order to balance the other two elected branches of government. The constitutional federal judges are, indeed, appointed by the president with the advice and consent of the Senate. The founders chose that approach precisely because they did not want judges to run for office and have to run again after issuing possibly unpopular decisions; they wanted them to be as apolitical as possible. Alexander Hamilton was of the view that periodic appointments, or terms of years, as distinguished from initial appointment and lifetime tenure, would be fatal to the independence of the judiciary. He warned:

> If the power of making them [periodic appointments] was committed either to the Executive or legislature, there would be danger of an improper complaisance to the branch which possessed it; if

to both, there would be an unwillingness to haz-
ard the displeasure of either; if to the people, or to
persons chosen by them for the special purpose,
there would be too great a disposition to consult
popularity, to justify a reliance that nothing would
be consulted but the Constitution and the laws.[1]

Federal judges are chosen by presidential nomination and Senate confirmation. The problems with
this process center on the partisanship involved in the
selection and confirmation. Chalk it up to the Internet, national polarity, or spillover from state judicial
selection battles, but the federal process has become
an increasingly visible and rancorous battleground.
Chief Justice Roberts decries the practical impact on
the judiciary:

> Over many years…a persistent problem has devel-
> oped in the process of filling judicial vacancies.
> Each political party has found it easy to turn on a
> dime from decrying to defending the blocking of
> judicial nominations, depending on their chang-
> ing political fortunes. This has created acute diffi-
> culties for some judicial districts. Sitting judges in
> those districts have been burdened with extraor-
> dinary caseloads…There remains, however, an
> urgent need for the political branches to find a
> long-term solution to this recurring problem.[2]

Partisanship has always pervaded the federal
selection process—indeed, the Constitution builds in
some wrangling between the executive and legislative
branches by requiring presidential nomination and
Senate confirmation. But collateral damage might be

on the rise. As the 2011 Defense Research Institute (DRI) report points out:

> The increased partisan wrangling over judicial appointments also contributes to the perception that the federal judiciary is not an independent branch of government that is "above the fray" of politics. And this perception brings with it skepticism and a lessening of respect for judicial rulings. Indeed, one senator attributed the rise in courtroom violence to increased politicization of the judiciary.[3]

There are some possible solutions to the problem. One approach is the use of bipartisan nominating committees, which is a procedure that has been in use in some states on an episodic basis over time. In 2008, the American Bar Association's House of Delegates unanimously passed Resolution 118, which recommends bipartisan commissions be established, at the state level for federal trial court vacancies and at the federal level for court of appeals vacancies, to help senators and the president fill vacancies[4] and to reduce "partisan tensions" in the nominating process.[5] There are various ways to choose members for such commissions, and their procedures can mirror nominating committees used in merit selection states. The use of such committees has the potential for watering down the partisanship and perceived political cronyism.[6]

Another possible solution is to establish a time period within which the Senate must act to confirm or deny the president's nominee, and if it fails to do so within that period, the nomination would automatically be deemed accepted.[7] That approach would, at the very least, allow the process to avoid gridlock along the way.

But just as the problem is circular, so too is the solution. If the American public and their elected representatives can stop thinking of judges as politicians or political operatives, then the institutionalization of nonpartisan processes to select those judges can begin to take deeper root.

Not all judicial officers in the federal system undergo political appointment. There are approximately 350 bankruptcy judges and 570 full- and part-time magistrate judges who largely operate under the political radar, and their selection process tends to be based on qualifications and performance. The bankruptcy and magistrate judges are not Article III judges (i.e., they are not appointed by the president with Senate confirmation, and they do not enjoy lifetime tenure). Bankruptcy judges are appointed by majority vote of active court of appeals judges and serve fourteen-year renewable terms. Their caseload is evident: they handle all of the bankruptcy cases in the nation. Magistrate judges are appointed by a majority vote of active district court judges and serve eight-year renewable terms. Magistrate judges have varying duties, depending upon the district in which they serve. They are nonconstitutional judicial officers who can and do handle major portions of the docket in many districts, and in other districts they handle primarily settlement conferences, preliminary matters in criminal cases, and pretrial discovery.

Moving to the state courts, judicial selection systems are a hodgepodge. Only one state has lifetime judicial appointment that mirrors the federal system; in several others, judges serve to an established mandatory retirement age. All the rest have systems that range across a spectrum from outright election of judges on partisan ballots to appointment and reappointment. In the middle is a system known variously as the "Missouri Plan," because it was first used in Missouri in 1940, or the "merit system."

This variety in judicial selection systems in the states was not always the case. Originally, the state selection systems mirrored the federal system in that judges were appointed to the judiciary for life. During the Jacksonian era in the nineteenth century, states changed to a system of electing their judges. This period of time, politically, was marked by the notion that the voice of the people was primary and by a mistrust of government institutions. There are numerous (and often debated) reasons for the political climate of this period that are not related to judicial selection. But the effect was a move toward outright election of judges. It seemed like a good idea at the time, but the bloom was soon off the rose in the minds of some observers. In his 1906 speech "Causes of Popular Dissatisfaction with the Administration of Justice," Roscoe Pound (later dean of Harvard Law School) lamented that "putting courts into politics and compelling judges to become politicians in many jurisdictions has almost destroyed the traditional respect for the Bench."[8] In the twentieth century, states began the move back to appointment and/or nonpartisan election, but have done so in fits and starts.

Despite this earlier trend, a majority of states today still do hold elections for their state court judges, and in our view, it is a problem. A big problem. Consider some fiction that is actually based on fact: the plot of John Grisham's novel *The Appeal*. An industrialist's company suffers a huge verdict in a civil suit over a pollution-related cancer cluster. He is then approached by an ideological cabal that persuades him to serve as the secret sugar daddy for a business-friendly candidate to unseat an incumbent on the state supreme court. The idea is to tip the balance on the court before the appeal of the verdict gets there. A mercenary political consultant explains the setup to the aspiring buyer of a seat on the bench:

> "We do campaigns. Have a look." He picked up a remote and pushed the button, and a large white screen dropped from the ceiling and covered most of a wall, then the entire nation appeared. Most of the states were in green, the rest were in a soft yellow. "Thirty-one states elect their appellate and supreme court judges. They are in green. The yellow ones have the good sense to appoint their courts. We make our living in the green ones."
>
> "Judicial elections."
>
> "Yes. That's all we do, and we do it very quietly. When our clients need help, we target a supreme court justice who is not particularly friendly, and we take him, or her, out of the picture."
>
> "Just like that."
>
> "Just like that."[9]

Everything about this Grisham tale is supposed to be shocking. In fact, it comes straight from the headlines. Grisham's story is derived from the twists and turns of a true story that resulted in a decade-long legal battle that reached the Supreme Court in 2009 and contains deeply disturbing events that seem like fiction but are becoming all too common in real life.

The real-life case involved Hugh Caperton, a small-businessman whose family has been in the coal business in West Virginia for a long time. His company,

Harman Development Corporation, filed a case against the much larger A. T. Massey Coal Company, alleging that Massey had systematically forced Harman out of business by creating circumstances that deprived Harman of a buyer either for their coal or for their business. Harman's argument was that Massey undertook that course of action in order to secure the business of a large coal buyer that had previously contracted with Harman. Caperton ultimately convinced a West Virginia jury of the correctness of his company's allegations, and he obtained a $50 million compensatory and punitive damage verdict against Massey in 2002.

At this point the story begins to sound more like a Grisham novel than a court case. As the appeal of the verdict was taking shape, Don Blankenship, the CEO of Massey Energy, donated $3 million to a committee that supported the campaign of Brent Benjamin, a then little-known candidate for the West Virginia Supreme Court of Appeals. The contribution accounted for some 60 percent of the overall spending on the campaign. Benjamin won the election and became a justice on that court.

Three years later, when the case came before the West Virginia Supreme Court of Appeals, Justice Benjamin dismissed the plaintiff's argument that he should disqualify himself from the case. Then he voted to overturn the $50 million jury verdict against Massey. Massey won the case by a vote of 3–2.

Caperton argued that he had been denied a fair appeal. The US Supreme Court accepted the case, and Caperton was represented by Theodore B. Olson, US solicitor general under George W. Bush and one of the most respected trial lawyers in the country. Olson summarized the complaint for the high court:

The improper appearance created by money in judicial elections is one of the most important issues facing our judicial system today. A line needs to be drawn somewhere to prevent a judge from hearing cases involving a person who has made massive campaign contributions to benefit the judge.[10]

In June 2009, the US Supreme Court voted 5–4 that the appearance of bias caused by the contribution invalidated the ruling.[11] Associate Justice Anthony Kennedy wrote that Justice Benjamin's failure to recuse himself had created an unconstitutional "probability of bias." In the dissent, Chief Justice John Roberts foreshadowed the thorny questions we now face: What's the threshold of monetary influence? What are the time limits of such conflicts? Should the recusal mandate apply only when a party contributes to a judge's campaign? What about when a person actively opposes rather than supports the judge—does that require recusal? And so on. What seems a simple proposition that justices should avoid even the appearance of a conflict of interest has turned out to be much more complex, and the Caperton case has spawned a debate across the nation about the appropriate contours of rules requiring a judge to step aside when a case involves a campaign contributor.

Consider Alabama. Candidates for the Alabama Supreme Court raised $4.3 million in their 2010 campaigns—more than in any other state. The Alabama legislature enacted a law that requires an appeals court judge who received more than $4,000 in campaign contributions from a litigating party in a case to step down in that case. The legislature told the Alabama

Supreme Court to adopt rules implementing the law. A panel, appointed by the court, concluded that there were too many problems with the law and recommended that it be retooled or repealed.

Maybe the panel was right; maybe the lines *are* too hard to draw. But the real question here should not be how much money it takes to trigger an appearance of bias; the question should be *why* we are forcing our judges to run this gauntlet at all. Selecting judges by contested elections invites conflict of interest. Instead of splitting hairs about how to minimize or correct those conflicts, we should change the system. Election of judges makes some intrinsic sense—in a perfect world. By that view, judges stay in touch with the voters and do not become isolated or removed because, after all, they have to campaign. More to the point, citizens do have a right to pick judges, and judges have a responsibility to be accountable to the citizenry. Elected judges can be more responsive to attorneys, journalists who need information, and even legislators. In a less politicized climate, election of judges might have accomplished all of those objectives with few downsides. This is not that climate. This climate is, in fact, a score of latitudinal zones away from that balmy ideal and precisely the sort of climate in which the Missouri Plan was born and in which states began moving away from contested judicial elections.

Missouri adopted the change in response to the undue influence and control of judicial selection by political machines and party bosses. Former president of the Bar Association of Metropolitan St. Louis William W. Crowdus described the situation in Missouri before 1940 with a caveat, saying he didn't mean to imply "that we did not have some excellent judges under our former system, but those good ones were such not on account of our old political system, but in spite of it."[12] Crowdus has numerous examples of the quality (or lack thereof) of the judges who did not fit within this caveat, such as Judge Eugene Padberg, "who stepped literally from the pharmacy to the bench," having only participated in nine lawsuits before becoming a pharmacist at a local hospital and then a judge.[13] His judicial candidacy was secured on account of his relationship with the boss of his political party, Crowdus explains, and, as expected, his record was "a travesty on justice"—so much so that a fellow judge resigned, "stating he had no longer [a] desire to remain a judge under the political system."[14]

In Colorado, the move to a merit selection system was prompted by the outcome of the 1954 general election, during which, according to Colorado Supreme Court Justice Gregory Hobbs Jr., "the toll electoral politics can take on a sitting judge for making one unpopular decision demonstrated itself dramatically."[15] The opinion at issue, authored by then chief justice Mortimer Stone, involved water rights and held that Denver's Dillon Reservoir on the Blue River was junior in priority to the Green Mountain Reservoir. In response to the court's 4–3 ruling—specifically, Chief Justice Stone's written opinion—the Denver Water Department campaigned aggressively and successfully against Chief Justice Stone at the next election. Justice Hobbs writes that this "raw example of how to beat a judge who decides against you" and the intimidation others felt should similar fates befall them led the Colorado Bar Association and other interested organizations to push for a move from elections to merit selection.[16] The constitutional amendment was approved by voters in 1966.

Although evidence of costly judicial campaigns began to surface in the 1990s, full-blown judicial selection wars are really a twenty-first-century phenomenon. Oregon state court judge Henry Kantor lays much of this at the feet of the public reaction to *Bush v. Gore*: "That galvanized a sort of subconscious way many people were thinking about the bench, that it was just a power play."[17] Another demarcation point was the US Supreme Court's 2002 decision in *Republican Party of Minnesota v. White*. Prior to that case, states with elections had provisions that prohibited a judicial candidate from expressing opinions during a campaign on issues that might come before the judge once elected. In *White*, the US Supreme Court held that those provisions were an unconstitutional abridgement of the candidate's freedom of speech: "There is an obvious tension between the article of Minnesota's popularly approved Constitution which provides that judges shall be elected, and the Minnesota Supreme Court's [rule] which places most subjects of interest to the voters off limits."[18] The case opened the door for judicial candidates to speak freely about their personal positions on controversial social issues, increasing pressure on candidates to make their views known even when they do not wish to do so. Special interest groups sent questionnaires to judicial candidates in, among other states, Iowa in 2006 and Florida in 2006 and 2008 asking for their positions on issues such as same-sex marriage, abortion, and assisted suicide. Questionnaires circulated in 2008 in Florida asked, for example,[19]

- Do you agree with the following statement? "The Florida Constitution recognizes a right to same-sex marriage."

- *Lofton v. Kearney*…held that a Florida law pro-
  hibiting homosexual adoption does not violate the
  Equal Protection Clause of the U.S. Constitution.
  Do you agree with this holding?

Campaign fund-raising has more than doubled in
the last two decades—from $83.3 million in the 1990s
to $206.9 million this past decade (excluding 2010).[20]
Furthermore, outside spending by noncandidate groups
has also increased dramatically in recent judicial elections[21]—seen most vividly in Iowa in 2010, where the
American Family Association (based in Mississippi),
Family Research Council (based in Washington, DC),
the National Organization for Marriage (also based in
Washington, DC), and others spent more than $1 mil-
lion to oust (successfully) three Iowa Supreme Court
justices for an opinion they joined on same-sex marriage.[22] Business and conservative groups were reported
to have spent more than lawyer and union counterparts
in every state with the exception of Illinois, where funding in 2010 for Justice Thomas Kilbride came in large
part from plaintiffs' lawyers, unions, and the Illinois
Speaker of the House.[23] Justice at Stake—a national
nonpartisan campaign to keep state and federal courts
fair and impartial—and the Brennan Center for Justice report that between August and October 2010,
noncandidate groups were the top spenders in four of
the five top-spending states, with Michigan and Ohio
offering the greatest disparity between candidate and
noncandidate spending.[24]

Even in the lower court races, where the big dollars are not as evident, judges frequently must make
"voluntary" political party contributions to get their
name on the ballot. The price of a trial court seat

in one midwestern state is estimated to be between $80,000 and $150,000.[25]

In 2000, candidates used television ads in contested supreme court elections in only four out of eighteen states with contested supreme court races.[26] By 2006, they were used in ten of eleven states, and in 2010 they were used in fourteen states.[27] And the tenor of those ads is chilling.

These factors have resulted in judicial campaigns that are expensive, scandalous, and misleading. Outside of the United States, judges must often pass rigorous tests and are selected based on technical skill. They are also generally appointed by an executive branch official. It's no wonder the rest of the world "is stunned and amazed at what we do, and vaguely aghast," according to Mitchel Lasser, an expert on international judicial systems.[28] In 2008, the *Economist* dubbed one judicial campaign a "habeas circus."[29] The campaign that gave rise to that telltale descriptor occurred in Wisconsin in 2008. It featured a series of disturbing television ads run by Michael Gableman against incumbent justice Louis Butler. The ads featured a deep and ominous female voice-over, with mentions of a rapist and crime scenes more reminiscent of a promotion for the latest *CSI* episode than a supreme court election. One ad alleged that "Louis Butler worked to put criminals on the street, like Reuben Lee Mitchell, who raped an 11-year-old girl with learning disabilities. Butler found a loophole. Mitchell went on to molest another child."[30]

Using the same dirty trick as the notorious Willie Horton ad of the 1988 presidential campaign, the television commercial included the African American perpetrator's mug shot. But the ad failed to acknowledge that the Mitchell case arose while Butler was a public defender—*before* he had ever become a judge—and that the crime occurred *after* the convicted rapist had served time in prison and been paroled. The ads in that campaign were so repugnant and misleading that broadcast stations eventually refused to air them. Several months after his win, these words came back to haunt Justice Gableman, who became the only Wisconsin judge to date to face state judicial commission charges that he made false statements about his opponent. Yet a panel of three appeals court judges found "no lie" and recommended that the case be dismissed. A victim of such ads, Justice Butler lost his seat in 2008, becoming the first incumbent justice in Wisconsin to do so in forty years.

This was not the only record set during the campaign. Nearly $6 million was raised to contest the seat—the biggest war chest the state had ever seen in a judicial election—and the lion's share of contributions came from groups outside the state. Under Wisconsin law, these contributors were not required to provide information about how they raised the money or spent it. Campaign watchers initially dubbed Wisconsin the poster child for the worst election antics of 2008, although a half dozen other states also vied for this dubious honor, including

- Alabama, where spending for one supreme court seat exceeded $4 million, with most of it going to sensational advertising that was so disturbing that both candidates were hauled before the state Judicial Campaign Oversight Committee.[31]
- Michigan, where voters were treated to the spectacle of what more than $3.6 million will buy in

advertising.[32] Ads in support of the incumbent chief justice alleged that his challenger granted a lenient sentence to a sex predator. Not to be outdone, his opponent aired a video reenactment alleging that the chief justice fell asleep during a case involving the deaths of six children in a house fire. This ad has been credited with the defeat of the chief justice, the first incumbent judge in that state to lose his seat in twenty-four years.

- Mississippi and Louisiana, where supreme court races broke records for advertising dollars spent and sank to new lows in the level of rhetoric. One Mississippi justice alleged that his opponent was a deadbeat dad; the accused fired back with an ad depicting judges with dollar signs on their chests, with the inference that justice came with a price tag. Another justice was the subject of an ad claiming he ruled in favor of two "baby killers."

These trends continued in the 2010 elections.

- In Alabama, a justice seeking votes in a state race used a recent federal decision to make his point. He alleged that a federal judge was as dangerous as Al Qaeda because of her decision in a case involving "don't ask, don't tell."[33] Talk about inflammatory hyperbole. Alabama is also notable in that no other state reached the level of individual fund-raising undertaken in the three judicial races—totaling $4.3 million.[34]
- Michigan, on the list again, received the honor of most expensive state supreme court campaign, with candidates raising a total of $2.7 million and outside spending on television ads totaling $5.1 million.[35]

In April 2011, Wisconsin hit the news (again) when the Wisconsin Supreme Court election between incumbent justice David Prosser and challenger JoAnne Kloppenburg became a tawdry battle-by-proxy over Wisconsin's recently enacted and controversial organized labor law. Third-party groups spent $4.5 million[36]—the biggest spenders were the Greater Wisconsin Committee, the Issues Mobilization Council of Wisconsin Manufacturers and Commerce, and Citizens for a Strong America.[37] The candidates themselves participated in the state's public financing program and received $400,000 each.[38]

The campaign featured a television ad that was labeled the "Mother of All Negative Ads."[39] It depicts Justice Prosser as a prosecutor in the late 1970s, shielding from prosecution a Catholic priest accused of molestation. The campaign also exposed bitter internal divisions within the court that stemmed from its handling of ethical allegations against a sitting justice who aired a similarly misleading ad during his 2008 campaign. No one came out of the process unscathed—least of all the public trust and confidence in the system.

At the very least, these smear campaigns have undermined the public's respect for the judiciary. According to a 2006 survey by the Annenberg Public Policy Center, although 65 percent of respondents expressed a preference for electing their judges rather than having them be nominated by governors, 70 percent nevertheless believed having to raise money for election campaigns affects a judge's ruling to a moderate or great extent.[40] Furthermore, 63 percent of respondents thought that pressure from past contributors would affect a judge's fairness and impartiality to either a moderate or great extent.[41] A 2007 Annenberg

survey shows that Americans who live in states that
hold partisan elections are more likely to agree with
the statement that "judges are just politicians in robes"
than those who live in states with some other selection
method.[42] This survey reaffirmed the 2006 Annenberg
study, finding that 69 percent of citizens believe that
raising campaign contributions affects a judge's rulings—either moderately or greatly.[43] A 2010 Harris
Interactive survey commissioned by Justice at Stake
found that "71 percent of Democrats and 70 percent
of Republicans believe campaign expenditures have a
significant impact on courtroom decisions," with only
23 percent of those surveyed believing such expenditures have little or no influence.[44]

Participating in a 2008 conference that focused
on the judicial selection debate, Justice O'Connor
revealed a conversation that she had with a group of
"top-notch" lawyers in Texas. The lawyers admitted
to a policy of researching the opposing counsel's campaign contributions to the judge; they then matched
the donations dollar for dollar. Justice O'Connor
lamented, "Judicial independence is a bedrock principle of our court system, and we're losing it."[45] She
concluded, "We've put cash in the courtroom, and it's
just wrong."[46] At best, campaign contributions have
corroded public trust. At worst, they are actually
affecting outcomes.

A 2002 Justice at Stake national bipartisan survey
shows that one in four judges (26 percent) themselves
believe that campaign contributions have at least some
influence on their decisions.[47] A Greenberg Quin-
lan Rosner Research and American Viewpoint survey in 2001–2002 found that 76 percent of Americans
believe that campaign contributions influence judicial

decisions and 46 percent of state court judges agreed.[48] In a 2010 Justice at Stake survey of West Virginia voters, 78 percent of those surveyed said that campaign contributions made to supreme court candidates have a great deal of, or some, influence on their decisions in court cases.[49] Richard Neely, a former elected judge of the West Virginia Supreme Court of Appeals, candidly admitted that "as long as I am allowed to redistribute wealth from out-of-state companies to injured in-state plaintiffs, I shall continue to do so. Not only is my sleep enhanced when I give someone else's money away, but so is my job security, because the in-state plaintiffs, their families, and their friends will reelect me."[50]

Economists Alexander Tabarrok and Eric Helland sampled more than fifty thousand tort cases from 1988 to 1996 and found that average awards against out-of-state businesses are $663,410 higher in states that hold partisan elections for judges as compared with those in which judges are appointed or that hold nonpartisan elections.[51] (Out-of-state companies don't vote.) Additionally, political scientists Gregory Huber and Sanford Gordon studied Pennsylvania trial judges in the 1990s and found that the closer those judges were to reelection, the harsher their sentences in criminal cases tended to be.[52]

In the words of late Massachusetts Supreme Court Justice Henry Lummus, "There is no certain harm in turning a politician into a judge. He may be or become a good judge. The curse of the elective system is the converse: that it turns almost every judge into a politician."[53]

These results should please neither conservatives nor liberals. One candid businessman said, "If I could buy every judge in the nation, I probably would. But,

I cannot—at the very least, there will be anti-business judges in 50 percent of the courtrooms, and with my luck, those are the courtrooms in which I will find my cases. I would prefer impartiality to a 50 percent chance of a judge who is biased against me."[54]

Aside from the ethical issues implicated by judicial elections, serious logistical issues arise far more frequently in jurisdictions with contested judicial elections. Consider Harris County, Texas, where in 2008 presiding judge Mark Davidson lost his retention election. For four years prior, Judge Davidson had served as the asbestos multidistrict litigation pretrial judge in the 11th District Court. Overnight, the multiple plaintiffs and defendants involved in the case lost the judge who had spent the last four years becoming familiar with the issues in the case and resolving pretrial disputes. To put this one example into perspective, in the 2006 Dallas County elections, all forty-two incumbent judges in contested races were unseated.[55] In Harris County two years later, twenty-two judges were unseated in the election.[56] The trend continued in 2010.[57] The docket and the litigants were the collateral damage.

It is not only how judges are selected that is critical to the integrity of the civil justice system—it is also how well they perform. Measurements are a relatively new concept in the court world; however, as case management guru Ernie Friesen has often said, "what you count, counts." Thus, through measurements, we encourage certain behaviors. And, yes, judges, too, can be subject to job performance evaluations. The message of judicial performance evaluation is that we value a certain kind of judge who will score well on a matrix related to judicial performance and professionalism. The message of judicial elections is that we value a judge who can raise money and put together a successful ad campaign. Which judge would you like to draw for your divorce or promissory note case?

Is there a way then to restore impartiality to the courtroom? We think so. It is judicial selection based on a merit system and a probationary period that still allows for elections but avoids the problems of campaigning and fund-raising. Our vision for the future of judicial selection is a four-step process, the O'Connor Judicial Selection Plan.

That process involves an open, balanced, and transparent (all meetings public) nominating commission (appointed for staggered terms by different appointing authorities and consisting of a majority of nonlawyers) that recommends highly qualified applicants to the governor. The governor then appoints a judge from the list of recommended names for a provisional term of office. During that provisional term, the judge is fully evaluated by a judicial performance evaluation (JPE), and at the end of that provisional term, the judge's name is on the ballot with an up/ down option afforded to the voters. The voters also have access to a compilation of JPE information. The judge runs on his or her performance record rather than on campaign ads or stump promises.

Here is how the four-step plan works in Colorado. When a vacancy occurs in a Colorado state court, a nominating commission takes applications: a state commission for appellate court vacancies, a local commission for trial court vacancies. Membership on these commissions is diverse and balanced. Fifteen members serve on the state commission, and only seven of them attorneys. The district commissions consist of four nonattorneys and three attorneys. At both levels, the nonattorneys are appointed by the governor and the attorney members are jointly appointed by the governor, attorney general, and chief justice of the supreme court. These commissions consider applicants for the judgeship and then recommend several names to the governor for possible appointment.

Once appointed, the individual selected by the governor serves an initial term of two years, and then must stand for retention at the next general election. In advance of this election, the Commissions on Judicial Performance undertake judicial performance evaluations of judges standing for retention, meaning the state commission reviews performance of court of appeals judges and Colorado Supreme Court justices, while the local district commissions review district and county judges. Each commission is composed of ten commissioners, again, six of whom are nonattorneys. Commissioners are appointed to four-year terms by the chief justice, the governor, the president of the Senate, and the Speaker of the House, respectively.

As part of the evaluation process, the commissions survey persons who have appeared before the judge, observe the judge in the courtroom, have the judge conduct a self-evaluation, and review decisions and relevant statistics. Shortly before the election, the Colorado Office of Judicial Performance Evaluation releases this evaluation, along with a recommendation of "retain," "do not retain," or "no opinion." If the voters vote to retain, the judge will then serve a full term, standing for retention again at the expiration of that term.

Only a handful of states (mostly western mountainous states) have the full four-step system in place for all judges in the state, but about half the states have a combination of processes that include appointment, commission-based selection and evaluation, and retention elections.[58]

The integrity of the O'Connor Judicial Selection Plan starts with the integrity of the nominating commission process. In order to avoid the appearance or the reality of a backroom special-interest selection process, the nominating commissions must be transparent and balanced. Citizens must have both a voice in and a window into the proceedings. Speaking of his participation on the Indiana Commission on Judicial Qualifications as one of the three laypeople on the commission (together with three attorneys), Daryl Yost found that the mix of attorney and nonattorney members "provided a forum for rich and enlightening dialogue."[59] Also, no one political party or interest group can be allowed to capture the commission. Yost reports that because the commission was never given any directives from the Indiana governor, he "felt unencumbered to satisfy a political influence."[60] He further notes that he did not experience lobbying from special interest groups.

Iowa, Kansas, and Missouri are making moves toward transparency in the process. After the 2010 elections, the Iowa State Judicial Nominating Commission opened the nominating process for the vacancies on the Iowa Supreme Court, making applicant information available on the commission's website along with live-streaming applicant interviews. In September 2010, Missouri opened the interviews of appellate court candidates to the public. A similar move was made in Kansas by the Kansas Supreme Court Nominating Commission. Transparency is one criteria identified by the US Chamber of Commerce Institute for Legal Reform to preserve the "merit" in merit selection: "The procedures that determine how state judges are selected and placed on the bench, particularly those in the highest courts, are central to the ultimate quality of justice in our courts."[61]

The judge of this author pair lived in that system for twenty years—first as a trial court judge and later as a member of the Colorado Supreme Court. Justices of the court serve as ex officio chairs of the district nominating commissions around the state. Eleven years of performing this role provided some insights. First, during that eleven-year period (serving as chair for at least twenty commission proceedings), only once was the question of an applicant's political affiliation raised. That sounds absolutely incredible, but it is true. It is possible that since the commissions were local, the commissioners already knew the politics of the various applicants. However, it is much more likely that those individual commissioners were thinking about choosing someone before whom they would be willing to appear in court—not someone who shared their politics. Granted, the political considerations might only really pop up at appellate court levels. However, the appellate nominating commission in Colorado regularly nominates three candidates with balanced political affiliations.

One fear when there is a majority of lawyer-commissioners is that they will dominate the process and choose judicial applicants who share their particular side of the "v." Thus, the perception is that plaintiffs' lawyer commissioners try to nominate applicants who are pro-plaintiff and defense lawyer commissioners nominate applicants who are pro-defendant. The O'Connor Judicial Selection Plan in fact supports a majority of *non*lawyers on nominating commissions to avoid any possibility of that bias and, equally importantly, the appearance of that bias. Remember that our focus is to reorient the system to the needs of the real users, not the lawyers. The individuals whose money, children, or lives are at issue before the judges have a much greater stake than the lawyers who act as counsel to those individuals—and they deserve a fair representation on the commissions. As a matter of personal experience, the lawyers on nominating commissions do sometimes dominate the questioning but seldom dominate the decision process. All of the commissioners recognize the importance of the choice they are making and, like jurors, take it very seriously.

Another critical component is judicial performance evaluation, a state-sanctioned program that collects and distributes certain data on how a judge is actually performing on the job. JPE is not a bar poll or a popularity contest. Rather, JPE involves canvassing a wide variety of individuals who have personal experience with a given judge (from jurors, litigants, law enforcement personnel, witnesses, and attorneys to other judges and court staff). Specifically, the questions focus on criteria such as level of preparation for hearings, knowledge of the law, efficiency, demeanor, clarity of orders and opinions, and timeliness. The information is supplemented by docket and case processing numbers and, in some states, by trained court-watcher reports or public hearing outcomes. In our view, the information needs also to include the judge's willingness to manage discovery appropriately, handle a case from start to finish, hold jury trials when warranted, and become familiar with the legal or factual complexities of the case. These measures have a variety of functions: they provide information to the judges themselves, they provide information to the voters, and they set what social scientists call a "normative" model for judicial behavior. In short, JPE is to judges what job evaluations are to every other worker who must meet an employer's expectations. Here, the people are the employers, and they expect a just, speedy, and inexpensive system.

Some form of officially sanctioned JPE is in place in at least a third of states around the country, but not in the federal system. This method of evaluating judges emerged in 1976 and was at first viewed with great skepticism by lawyers and judges alike who argued that justice is in the eye of the beholder and can never be measured. Over the intervening decades, JPE has gained ground as a way to achieve some of the objectives (e.g., accountability) of an election system without the taint of moneyed politics. Since 2005, the growth of JPE use nationwide has been strong and steady. Several states have introduced new JPE programs for judges at different levels, three states have developed JPE pilot projects, and two states have revised existing JPE programs to ensure greater comprehensiveness and transparency. In Colorado, where JPE has been in place for more than twenty years, the judges believe that the feedback they receive helps them improve and actually protects judicial independence because it quantifies and directs an analysis of what it takes to be a good judge.

Overall results suggest that some version of the O'Connor Plan or merit selection serves the public well. A 2010 survey conducted by Harris Interactive for the US Chamber of Commerce found that judges chosen through a merit selection system rank among the best in the nation.[62] The survey reported that six of the top ten states in rankings of judicial competence and seven of the top ten states in rankings of judicial impartiality use merit selection to pick their judges. Conversely, three out of the bottom five states ranked in judicial competence and four of the bottom five ranked in judicial impartiality use a partisan election system. All of the bottom five states in both categories elect judges—whether in partisan or nonpartisan elections. These trends are consistent over the eight-year period for which the US Chamber has collected data.

Given the tenor of judicial campaigns and the existence of an alternative that is reasonable, reform should be on the march. Historically, opposition to elimination of election systems has come more from the defense bar than the plaintiffs' bar; however, reasonable lawyers on both sides are now seeing the need for change. The Defense Research Institute—an international organization dedicated to the interests of business and individuals in civil litigation—reports that "the level of activity and commentary on judicial selection methods suggests that momentum may be developing for change designed to protect the independence of our judicial system."[63] An April 2011 National Center for State Courts special edition of *Gavel to Gavel* finds "little doubt that this is the single most active year with respect to merit selection in decades."[64] Former Indiana Commission on Judicial Qualifications member Daryl Yost reports: "I have become increasingly aware of the enormity of the task to change how [judges are selected]; however, I am convinced it *must* begin."[65] Major reform is never a straight line, but in this case it looks more like an eddy in the middle of the stream. Since 2006, five states have seriously evaluated a move from elections to merit selection. In 2008, Missouri voters affirmatively embraced an appointment/

retention model, and in both 2008 and 2010, voters
in Kansas staved off a move toward elections. In 2010,
Nevada was the first state since 1988 to have an initiative on the ballot to change the selection method for
all judges from election to an appointment/retention
system; sadly, the measure went down, 58 percent to
42 percent. This is in a state where corruption in the
judiciary had been documented. The reason cited most
often by voters for opposing the initiative was that they
did not want to lose their right to cast ballots. Echoing
the same refrain, a 2008 Harris Poll found that over
half of citizens surveyed still preferred direct election
of judges over any other method.[66] Or, as Judge Kantor puts it, "Folks want to know—even if they don't
exercise their franchise most of the time—that they can
throw the bums out."[67]

The subject of judicial selection is a front-burner
issue to court-watchers and perhaps politicians around
the country. A few states are considering a move to
appointment/retention; others are going the other
way, looking at moving from nonpartisan elections
to partisan elections. The question of Senate confirmation is under debate, as is a broader federal-type
approach. In short, there is movement, but with no
particular guiding principle other than dissatisfaction.

Other initiatives that are palliative measures
include campaign finance reform, public financing
of judicial campaigns, and efforts to strengthen recusal standards. For example, New York court administrators issued a proposed rule amendment in early
2011 that would prohibit the assignment of a judge
to a case where an attorney or a party had contributed
$2,500 to the judge's campaign within the previous
two years. Quoting New York chief justice Jonathan

Lippman, a proponent of the amendment, the *New York Law Journal* wrote that "the view that judges either are prohibited from learning about who their campaign contributors are, or manage to avoid finding out, even when attending their own fundraisers, is, 'Not really compatible with the society we live in today.'"[68] Although not commenting on the proposal, the New York State Bar Association has traditionally treated such proposals as bandages "that would not fix the fundamental problems of electing judges."[69]

At the end of the day, the debate over how America chooses its judges boils down to one very simple question: what kind of judges do we want? Millions of individuals and thousands of businesses find themselves in US courts every year. Anyone who enters a courtroom should have confidence that the judge is competent, respectful, fair, and, most importantly, impartial. Betting on the impartiality of judges who accept substantial campaign contributions, or who take positions in advance of hearing cases that could raise those very issues, is a gamble that no one should have to take.

3

The Importance of Trials

In *The Wisdom of Crowds*, James Surowiecki tells a story about the famously snobby nineteenth-century anthropologist Francis Galton.[1] A pioneer of surveys and statistics, Galton delighted in producing research that was designed to show the stupidity of the masses (no surprise that he coined the word *eugenics* and championed its practice). In this anecdote, however, Galton's arrogance receives a broadside. He is astonished when his poll of the crowd at a county fair reveals that their guesses as to the weight of a prize ox, when averaged, came to within *one pound* of the half-ton creature's actual weight. More to the point, the crowd's mean projection was closer than any of the individual estimates made by the attending "livestock experts." Hence the title of Surowiecki's book.

There truly is wisdom in crowds, despite all kinds of popular and vocal opinion to the contrary. Yes, history is filled with instances of chaos, lynch mobs, and kangaroo courts. Yes, the educated "elite" are often privy to more rarified information than the layperson. Yes, many legal experts and observers echo the sentiments of columnist Tim Cavanaugh, who wrote in *Reason Magazine* in 2005 that "American jurors are a bunch of louts, nincompoops, and media whores who need to stop trusting their guts and start listening to people smarter than themselves."[2]

But social science increasingly tells us otherwise. It tells us that reasonably informed crowds, organized under clear rules, more often than not lead us down the path to wisdom. And, even if their decisions are not shot through with wisdom, having juries in our courtrooms has its own wisdom.

When shaping our legal system, the Republicans and Federalists, Jeffersonians and Hamiltonians alike knew that. From the very start, they were deeply supportive of the jury trial for both criminal matters and substantive civil complaints. As the relatively centrist John Adams wrote in 1774, "Representative government and trial by jury are the heart and lungs of liberty. Without them we have no other fortification against being ridden like horses, fleeced like sheep, worked like cattle and fed and clothed like swine and hounds."[3]

Indeed, this is possibly what those who later drafted the Declaration of Independence, and then the US Constitution and its Bill of Rights, felt when the Crown began its steady assault on trial by jury in civil cases—examples of which include the Sugar Act (Revenue Act of 1764) and Stamp Act (Duties in American Colonies Act 1765), both of which stripped colonists of their right to a civil jury trial by giving jurisdiction of these cases to the admiralty courts. Although the Declaration of Independence listed the Crown's assault on juries as one of the injustices it perpetrated against the colonies, for various reasons the right to trial by jury in civil cases was initially left out of the US Constitution. "At least seven of the states ratifying the Constitution," however, "called for immediate amendment to secure the right" to civil jury trials.[4]

It was not long thereafter that Congressman James Madison presented the list of amendments he thought should be incorporated into a bill of rights, including that "in suits at common law, between man and man, the trial by jury, as one of the best securities to the rights of the people, ought to remain inviolate."[5] The Seventh Amendment became law in 1791. As Thomas Jefferson explained, juries were considered to be the antidote to authoritarian judges:

> We all know that permanent judges acquire an Esprit de corps, that being known they are liable to be tempted by bribery, that they are misled by favor, by relationship, by a spirit of party, by a devotion to the Executive or Legislative; that it is better to leave a cause to the decision of cross and pile, than to that of a judge biassed to one side; and that the opinion of 12 honest jurymen gives still a better hope of right, than cross and pile does. It is left therefore to the juries, if they think the permanent judges are under any biass whatever in any cause, to take upon themselves to judge the law as well as the fact. They never exercise this power but when they suspect partiality in the judges, and by the exercise of this power they have been the firmest bulwarks of English liberty.[6]

Jurors keep the system grounded and anchored in real life. They ensure that the system is about justice, as opposed to gamesmanship and process for the sake of process. In our increasingly complex world, they require litigants and their counsel to bring the disputes down to what is important, and they add transparency and sunshine to the legal system. Analogous to the notion that an author must take the time to make something short and simple, so too do attorneys and judges in jury trials have to take the time to synthesize the issues down to the most important questions for the jury. Juries do not forgive duplication, inefficiency, or deliberate obfuscation.

Apart from voting, serving on a jury is arguably the most profound way that citizens get to participate in government. Courts across the nation, however, are grappling with the issue of jurors failing to appear. In 2009, failure-to-appear rates for jury service averaged 9 percent, with some courts reporting rates as high as 50 percent.[7] This is problematic—if too few jurors appear, jury trials cannot be held. The National Center for State Courts reported that in 2008, judges in Colorado, Ohio, North Carolina, and Vermont were forced to pull random citizens from offices, businesses, and off the streets to serve.[8] In Weld County, Colorado, of the two hundred summonses sent, only thirty-nine citizens appeared to fulfill their jury duty on January 16, 2008.[9] The court responded by issuing an order authorizing court administrators to serve people on the streets with summonses to report to jury duty—immediately. This phenomenon might not necessarily reflect a general disregard for the courts and their function. Most citizens—even those who fail to respond to a jury summons—do take jury duty very seriously. In the late 1990s, the American Judicature Society conducted a study to examine the extent and causes of nonresponse to summonses. The survey data of summoned jurors indicated the following:

> The variations in attitudes toward juries, jury service, and the court by income, education, race,

and economic circumstances indicate that many of those who would greatly appreciate the opportunity to serve as a juror are prevented from doing so by personal and financial circumstances, while many of those who would bring substantial expertise to the courts are reluctant to do so because of the perceived inconvenience that the process of reporting for jury duty—*not the experience of serving on a jury*—would entail.[10]

Furthermore, the data suggested that the nonresponders to summonses were "not ignorant of the positive aspects of jury service or of the nature of the experience they would have as jurors."[11]

A more recent, broader survey of US adults confirms citizens' perceived importance of jury trials. According to a 2004 Harris Poll prepared for the American Bar Association, 84 percent of respondents agreed that jury duty is an important civic duty, even when it is inconvenient.[12] The rate of agreement is higher among respondents who have actually been called to serve on a jury; 87 percent agreed, compared to 80 percent of respondents who have not been called.[13] Three out of four said they would want a case of their own to be tried to a jury rather than a judge.[14]

In short, jury trials have a very important function in our way of government—maybe even more so now that civic education and civic involvement are on the wane. In a recent study, John Gastil, E. Pierre Deess, Philip J. Weiser, and Cindy Simmons found that "participating in the jury process can be an invigorating experience for jurors that changes their understanding of themselves and their sense of political power and broader civic responsibilities."[15] Gilbert

Dickinson, a defendants' medical malpractice lawyer in Colorado who has taken a leadership role nationally in underscoring the importance of jury trials (not always a popular opinion among defense lawyers, who have sometimes decried runaway juries), sums up the situation most aptly: "Juries represent the collective wisdom and objectivity of a group of citizens who are called together to apply their common sense and agree on a verdict. It is indispensible to our system of justice, and our way of life."[16]

Now, at the beginning of the twenty-first century, jury trials—especially in civil cases—are in trouble. Far from functioning as the heart and lungs of liberty, they are currently on life support. Citizens can no longer afford them. Increasingly, lawyers and judges don't know how to conduct them. It seems to be faster, cheaper, and easier on everybody to settle cases or to send them to arbitration than to try them (except that in many cases it's *not* faster or cheaper). Trials by juries, like trials in general, are in danger of becoming extinct.

In the last few years, the reality of the vanishing trial has been confirmed. As chronicled by University of Wisconsin law professor Marc Galanter in a seminal 2004 *Journal of Empirical Legal Studies* article, the decline in trials has not been gradual; it has been recent and steep. Galanter found that during the last half century, civil trials (both trials to a jury and to a judge) as a percentage of total dispositions in US district courts declined precipitously, from 11.5 percent in 1962 to 1.8 percent in 2002.[17] And the absolute number of jury trials in district courts also reached a new low in 2010, when the percentage of civil cases reaching trial was 1.1 percent of total cases.[18]

Furthermore, Galanter and Angela Frozena found that since the mid-1980s, the number of civil trials in district courts has fallen by every major case category (e.g., contract cases, tort cases, civil rights cases, intellectual property cases).[19] For the percentage of civil cases that reach trial by major case category, Galanter and Frozena found the steepest decline in contract and tort cases.[20] A growing portion of trials are in civil rights cases and prisoner petition cases, although in absolute numbers these categories are also declining.[21]

Fewer cases filed, perhaps? Hardly. Galanter reported that the number of civil filings in district courts has *increased* fivefold since 1962.[22] Likewise, per capita civil filings in district courts have also risen significantly.[23] In spite of the increase in the number of civil filings, the size of the population, and the size of the economy, recent data show that the number of *trials* is still declining. Based on a preliminary finding that the ratio of trials to filings as of 2009 was about one-twelfth what it was in 1962, Galanter and Frozena compared the American trial to the disappearing Cheshire cat from *Alice in Wonderland*.[24] The grin may be the last thing to go.

The trend holds true for state courts as well. Those courts, where the overwhelming majority of cases are filed, have seen a similar decline. A survey of twenty-two states in another 2004 *Journal of Empirical Legal Studies* article found that the number of civil jury trials decreased by 32 percent from 1976 to 2002.[25] The study's authors found this decline has not been matched by a decrease, as in federal courts, in civil case terminations, which doubled in these state courts between 1976 and 2002, or a decline in population, which increased during this time period by 39 percent.[26]

To put these numbers into perspective, in Colorado federal court, only 1.2 percent of civil cases went to trial (judge or jury) in 2010.[27] Ten years earlier, in 2000, 3.7 percent of civil cases went to trial.[28] By contrast, when Judge Henry Kantor first took the bench in Oregon state court in 1994, he conducted a jury trial on the first day he was sworn in.[29] There was also a time when "trial" attorneys used to try cases. Judge Joseph Anderson of the US District Court in the District of South Carolina points to veteran attorney Abraham Lincoln, who was reported to have tried three thousand civil and criminal cases during his legal career.[30] In the mid-1900s, South Carolina plaintiffs' attorney James P. "Spot" Mozingo was reported to have tried more than six hundred civil and criminal cases—all before the age of fifty-nine.[31] During two and a half years in the Alameda District Attorney's Office, now California Supreme Court Justice Ming Chin tried approximately fifty jury cases.[32] "Can you imagine?" relates a nostalgic Justice Chin. "What a great experience."[33]

The bottom line: we have more people and more cases, but many fewer jury trials. So why is this happening?

First, a lot of people think juries are unreliable, that they might "run away" with the verdict and punish deep-pocket defendants inappropriately. Empirically, this is just not true. Juries are not pro-plaintiff, nor can it be said that they are pro-defendant. In a review of tort cases decided by juries in the seventy-five most populous counties in the United States, plaintiffs prevailed on average in 51 percent of cases (the exact percentage varies by case type).[34] Actually, studies have also shown that juries are even a bit less pro-plaintiff than the judges presiding over those trials. In a seminal 1950s nationwide survey of the judges in four thousand state and federal civil jury trials that asked judges how they would decide those cases, the data showed a 78 percent agreement between judge and jury on liability.[35] In 10 percent of the cases in which they did not agree, the judge would have been more favorable to the plaintiff, and in 12 percent, the jury would have been more favorable to the plaintiff.[36] Pretty much a wash. Furthermore, plaintiffs in medical malpractice and product liability cases would have prevailed at trial at a much higher rate if the judge had been making the decision (48 percent) than they did with juries rendering the verdict (28 percent).[37]

In fact, data show that judges agree with juries at the same rate they agree with other judges. Moreover, the rate of agreement between judge and jury is better than the rate of agreement found between scientists doing peer review and psychiatrists and physicians when diagnosing patients.[38] It is even more significant when compared to the 79–80 percent rate of agreement that a mid-1980s study found to exist between judges themselves when making sentencing decisions in an experimental setting.[39] A study undertaken in the early 1990s of sixty-seven civil trials yielded rates of agreement similar to the 1950s survey, with the exception that in this later study, judges were somewhat more likely than the jury to find for the plaintiff.[40] As Galton's county fair attendees demonstrated, collective wisdom is likely to be on the mark.

So, the notion that runaway juries are commonplace is an urban myth. Moreover, when a verdict is inappropriate, the appeals process works it out. For example, we previously mentioned the renowned

McDonald's hot coffee verdict that started out at $200,000 in compensatory damages and $2.7 million in punitive damages, and was reduced by the trial court to $640,000. During the appeal, the parties settled for an undisclosed amount less than $600,000.[41] The system corrected for the jury's excess.

Another common misperception of juries is based on the assumption that jurors are incapable of understanding complex issues and the accompanying expert testimony; however, juries "use reasonable strategies to evaluate expert testimony," such as drawing on the experience and expertise of their members to make sense of the evidence and looking for cues relating to the trustworthiness or potential biases of the source.[42] One of the reasons jury trials are in decline might be because the pretrial process has supplanted the trial. In today's world, the likely course of a lawsuit is complaint and answer; discovery (and discovery disputes); motion for summary judgment; and settlement (if the motion is not granted in full). As jury trials have declined, "trial by paper" via summary judgment has risen. Research from the Institute for the Advancement of the American Legal System (IAALS) drilling into eight federal district courts during a one-year period spanning 2005 and 2006 shows that summary judgment motions were filed in 16.6 percent of cases.[43] A study conducted by the Federal Judicial Center— the research and education agency of the federal judicial system—of summary judgment in six federal district courts published in the *Journal of Empirical Legal Studies* found that the percentage of cases containing one or more summary judgment motions increased from 12 percent to 19 percent from 1975 to 1988.[44] The study found that summary judgment rates have remained fairly steady since then; however, there was an increase between 1975 and 2000 in the percentage of cases in which such motions were granted in whole or part—from 6 to 12 percent.[45] So motions for summary judgment are being filed at about the same rate, but they are now granted in whole or in part twice as often. Has summary judgment taken the place of trial by jury?

Even the words *summary judgment* are fighting words among plaintiff and defense attorneys. Plaintiffs' attorneys tend to think that summary judgment is overused and is a tool that defendants use to increase costs and drive cases toward settlement. Defense attorneys tend to think that summary judgment is an appropriate method of disposing of groundless litigation in a way that costs less than trial. Which is true? The data are not conclusive because they do not compare summary judgment costs to trial costs, but recent empirical studies do shine some light on how time-consuming and expensive summary judgment practice can be. The IAALS federal docket study found that across eight federal district courts, the median time from filing to ruling on summary judgment motions was 126 days, and in many districts the median time was considerably longer.[46] Added to the costs of actually briefing and responding to a motion for summary judgment is the delay that it causes. Time is money in litigation, so the longer the case goes on, the more it is likely to cost. The Federal Judicial Center's recent analysis of litigation costs in civil cases determined that any ruling on a summary judgment motion was associated with an increase of 24 percent in plaintiffs' reported costs and a 22 percent increase in defendants' reported costs.[47]

Another reason for the decline in trials is the funneling of civil cases into mediation, arbitration, or some other form of alternative dispute resolution (ADR) that is either annexed to the court or completely in the private realm. At the same time Galanter published evidence of the vanishing jury trial, Thomas Stipanowich, president of The International Institute for Conflict Prevention and Resolution (the CPR Institute), describes a "quiet revolution" in ADR. According to Stipanowich, because of "increasingly daunting litigation costs and perceived great risks, the great majority of major businesses were led to experiment with ADR."[48] Chief Judge Janice Davidson of the Colorado Court of Appeals laments: "It just sickens me to see ADR, which is a wonderful tool, reveal how many people can't afford to use the system. For the typical civil case, we're becoming almost irrelevant."[49] ADR and jury trials have been pitted against one another with the increased use of arbitration clauses in contracts, under which parties to the contract are bound to arbitrate, thereby eliminating the right to trial by jury. These contracts can include cell phone contracts, insurance contracts, or even employment contracts—in short, contracts everyone is likely to sign at some point. State courts have been split on how to interpret these clauses in light of the Seventh Amendment. Arbitration was viewed as the antidote to court cost and delay.

Increasingly, however, the attraction of arbitration is waning. It is testament to the comparative value of the trial system that more and more litigators, including those of the corporate defense variety, are finding arbitration plagued by the same cost inflation and procedural inefficiency from which they thought they had escaped. "Slowly but surely," says litigator Philip

G. Kircher, "what was once supposed to be fast and cheap was becoming probably just as expensive, if not more so, than going to court."[50] Arbitration is not the panacea we had expected, either in terms of saving money, saving time, or achieving fairness. Complex discovery, multilayered depositions, and aggressive tactics have become common there, too.

In fact, justice might be short-circuited when farmed out. Appeal rights are very limited, and parties might be stuck with an outcome that is just not fair by any standard. A Rand Corporation survey of select corporate counsel found that they "overwhelmingly believe that arbitrators tend to 'split the baby' with their rulings—that is, they are unwilling to rule strongly for one party."[51] Furthermore, paid by the hour and chosen in the first instance by the attorneys in the case, arbitrators do not have the institutional duty to be impartial and in fact might be acting with a view toward building a repeat clientele.

Francis P. Devine III, coleader of the Philadelphia law firm Pepper Hamilton's litigation and dispute resolution department, explains, "I think there are many people, and I'm included, who would prefer to try a case to [a judge or jury] and when the case is over you know the case is over...Arbitration can go on forever and ever."[52]

Are these processes really cheaper and faster than trial by jury? Or is it just more comfortable for the lawyers and the judges?

Two judges at a 2010 Federal Bar Association panel captured the essence of the divergent viewpoints on this question. Judge D. Brock Hornby of the District of Maine contends that the shift away from trials is due to forces from outside the judiciary, such as a move toward arbitration rather than court proceedings. He asserts that it is not necessarily a negative phenomenon, since many claims do actually turn on private concerns and don't involve the public interest. "We have to serve litigants and their lawyers in a way that meets their needs. As federal judges, we don't have a roving mandate to go out and bring cases in and compel people to go to trial."[53]

On the other hand, Judge William Young of the District of Massachusetts mourns the decline in trials and blames the judiciary, arguing that judges try to manage cases toward settlement, too often succeeding. Judges who were not themselves trial lawyers might seek to avoid trials because they are not comfortable presiding over a trial or because trials take too much time. If a case is set for trial and it settles, the judge is relieved—he or she can turn to the stack of pending motions on the desk. According to Judge Young, that approach undermines the true function of a judge. He would encourage judges to spend less time in chambers and more time on the bench resolving disputes in an open forum. US district court judge Jack Zouhary of the Northern District of Ohio echoes Judge Young's sentiments. "There is a sense among some judges," Judge Zouhary will tell you, "that a trial is a failure of the system. And if you don't settle a case, there is something wrong with what you're doing."[54] To Judge Zouhary, it is quite the opposite: "Affording parties the opportunity to settle is important, but equally important is affording them the opportunity to have their case timely tried."[55]

According to the *National Law Journal*, Judge Young's critique proceeds from the observation that two crucial elements are in free fall: (1) the number of hours most judges actually sit in the courtroom, and (2) the amount of money that most jurisdictions spend on juries. Judge Young noted that court records reveal that federal judges average only about 175 hours a year (approximately twenty-two days) presiding over hearings counted as trials.[56] "If we spend 10 percent or less of our time doing what it is the public thinks we do," he said, "our system is dysfunctional."[57] Instead, judges are resolving motions, addressing pretrial discovery disputes, and holding case management conferences. Judge Young advocates stricter enforcement of trial dates and more denials of continuances. He also makes the case for district-by-district publication of judges' bench times and more fluidity of judicial assignments so that administrators will be free to supplement busier districts.[58]

Judge Patrick Higginbotham of the US Court of Appeals for the Fifth Circuit notes the growth of a new shared legal community and culture in which fewer trials are held, fewer lawyers have trial experience, and fewer judges take the bench with trial experience. The days of trial attorneys who are experienced in handling a case from start to trial are over—litigators who conduct discovery, file motions, settle cases, and seldom if ever present their case to the jury have taken their place in front of the bench and on the bench. Similarly, as Yale law professor Judith Resnik has duly noted in coining the phrase "the managerial judge," too many judges might even be anti-trial. She, like Judge Zouhary, suggests that they view trials as failures and take the position that a bad settlement is better than a good trial.

The changing role of a judge as an administrator and the growth of ADR, among other things, are driving cases out of courtrooms. Resnik describes this process through the use of courthouse imagery, in which courtroom architecture designed to make space "that exemplifies the idea of law as accessible" stands in stark contrast to "what is happening in adjudicatory processes in the United States."[59] The result, writes Resnik, is that all too often one finds "the austere hallways of various grand courthouses on both the national and international levels...empty."[60]

There is some good news. Despite the fact that the number of jurors in many courthouses has been declining over the last few decades, during this same time there are jurisdictions in which juror-centered innovations have been a priority. In the early 1990s, under the leadership of courts in California and Arizona, courts across the nation began considering such changes. The underpinnings for these changes was captured in a short video that showed an Arizona judge acting as a professor in a class. The film begins with the professor explaining to the students that they will be in the class for an indeterminate period of time, may not take notes or talk to one another about the subject matter, and will not learn what the final exam will be about until the end, but their grade on the exam could change someone else's life. The demonstration made patently clear the nonsensical approach that courts had been taking to communicating with and to jurors, and it sparked real interest in change.

As of now, many state courts and a growing number of federal courts are committed to jury innovations, and it is an example of the system reinventing itself in order to accommodate the needs of users—in this instance, jurors. Innovations can relate to the process of jury service: online systems of assuring that the trial is going to proceed and that the jurors will be needed, parking and child care instructions. And, they relate to the operation of the trial itself: pre-instructing jurors on the nature of the issues in the case, allowing jurors to pose questions to witnesses, providing juror notebooks with exhibit copies and lists of witnesses, and rewriting jury instructions in understandable language. At the same time, the courts are still struggling mightily with how to handle jurors who use Twitter or Google while they are serving as jurors. Since jurors are sworn to make their decision on the basis of the evidence presented in the courtroom and not do their own research, and since jurors are not supposed to be talking to (or tweeting) anyone about the case until it is over, these issues are real and troubling. Retired judge Dennis M. Sweeney notes that "virtually every day there are new reports of jurors…imperiling trials through unauthorized or unwise use of electronic devices on the Internet."[61] These instances have become commonplace enough to have earned the descriptor "Google mistrial."[62] This modern wrinkle merely reinforces the basic duty to give jurors the best possible information for their decision-making process. The system must meet that promise—however the problem of tweets and Google searches is ultimately resolved.

The success of these innovations depends on the vitality of the jury trial itself. It would be too easy, says attorney and past president of the American College of Trial Lawyers David Beck, to "dismiss the phenomenon of the vanishing jury trial as simply the self-interested lamentations of trial lawyers looking to preserve their way of life."[63] Rather, we must consider "the *consequences* of the decline and the

resulting impact on our social institutions and individual rights."[64] The jury system is, as Thomas Jefferson noted, "the only anchor ever yet imagined by man,
by which a government can be held to the principles
of its constitution."[65] It is the one place where citizens
contribute directly to the administration of justice and
where they can gain a first-person understanding of
how the courts work in practice.

Jury trials are of deep and abiding historic importance to our social character. They are a hallmark of
our civil justice system and democratic government.
When the system has become so expensive and time-
consuming that plaintiffs and defendants cannot
afford to have their cases heard by juries—and when
jury boxes across the nation are empty, day after day—
the system is broken. Beck suggests the fundamental
question is this: "Do we want a judicial system of the
type to which we are being inexorably pushed?"[66] We
would say no.

4

Funding Justice and
Fostering Innovation

A ll portions of government are suffering budget crises. In that respect, the courts are no different. When it comes to courts, however, the hue and cry is quite muted, and the impact is underestimated. To counter this, first we want to drive home the ways in which underfunded courts can negatively impact our everyday lives. No money for courts? Who cares? You should.

Second, we want to suggest that the time for the rebuilding process is *now*—efficiencies and a new look at court operations are no longer the stuff of cocktail party conversations or isolated conferences. Rather, they are the lifeblood of the survival of the courts.

Federal courts are funded by Congress. Although they are in much better shape financially than state courts, as we will explain, they face a different financial issue: judicial pay. Chief Justice John Roberts— in his 2006 year-end report on the federal judiciary, dedicated entirely to this topic—referred back to his predecessor William Rehnquist's first year-end report more than twenty years ago, in which Justice Rehnquist focused on the inadequacy of judicial compensation (a topic he returned to throughout his time as chief justice). Two decades later, Chief Justice

Roberts reports that "the decline in real compensation has continued."[1]

Since 1991, the salaries of federal judges have increased by 39 percent while the cost of living has increased by more than 50 percent.[2] Contrast these numbers to the pay increase of other federal employees, which has increased 87 percent in the same time period.[3] Chief Justice Roberts reported that, compared to the American worker in general, average wages have risen 18 percent in real terms since 1969 while federal judicial pay has declined by 24 percent.[4]

It is not too surprising, therefore, that twice the number of federal judges left the bench in the last twenty years than left between 1958 and 1989.[5] The perspective from Chief Justice Roberts's position is that "in the face of decades of congressional inaction, many judges who must attend to their families and futures have no realistic choice except to retire from judicial service and return to private practice."[6] The American Bar Association offers further warning:

> If the problem of fair judicial compensation is not addressed soon, inadequate judicial salaries will negatively affect the ability of the judiciary to continue to attract the most qualified attorneys from all segments of the legal profession.[7]

The other related problem in the federal judiciary is empty seats that stay empty for far too long. For a variety of reasons (including resignation, retirement, and political stalling), there are a significant number of empty chairs weighing down the federal judiciary. For example, when Congress began its 2010 session, there were more than one hundred vacancies in federal courts across the nation.[8] However, of the forty-two nominees for the federal bench to fill these vacancies, as of February 2010 the Senate had only confirmed fifteen.[9]

Consider the effect of these vacancies on the everyday business of the courts. The US Judicial Conference categorizes judicial vacancies as "judicial emergencies" based primarily on the respective district's "weighted filings" per judgeship (a measure of the difficulty of the cases on the docket) and the amount of time the judgeship has been vacant. In early June 2011, twenty-seven district vacancies were "emergencies," as were eight court of appeals vacancies.[10] In his 2010 year-end report, Chief Justice Roberts pointed to the "persistent problem of judicial vacancies in critically overworked districts" as one of the immediate obstacles to achieving the goals of the judiciary: cost savings, improved efficiency, reduced backlogs, and increased public trust.[11]

In the state courts, the crisis of funding and workload is even more pervasive and pernicious. State courts are almost wholly funded through state, county, and local mechanisms. They receive their funding primarily from taxes on sales, income, and property. Funding is spread across state, county, and municipalities. But the relationship between state courts and the holders of the purse strings is dicey. Judges or their administrative counterparts have to go to the funding entities annually to request budget allocations—this, for a separate and co-equal branch of government, seems problematic. The "hat in hand" analogy is the one that comes to mind, and it does not sit particularly well with the courts.

To be sure, judges' salaries are an inflammatory subject, particularly when judges seek salary increases in the wake of controversial decisions, but the larger question is the budget for court operations overall. The allocations are plummeting, and no end is in sight. Budgets in eleven state courts in fiscal year 2010 were cut in excess of 5–8 percent, three state courts experienced 9–12 percent budget decreases, and three state courts suffered budget decreases of 12 percent or more.[12] And the next fiscal year looms dark on the horizon. Many more courts will suffer deep cuts, given state budget realities. This is occurring at a time when Americans are asking more and more of those same courts—civil case filings in state trial courts increased by 2.7 million from 2005 to 2008.[13] Clerks' office staff is being cut, and court hours are being decreased. As of December 2010, sixteen states have enacted furloughs of clerical and administrative staff with reductions in pay, nine states have enacted furloughs and pay reductions for judicial officers, fifteen states have reduced hours of operation, and fourteen states have laid off staff.[14]

The effect is that in courts across the nation, judges are carrying increasingly heavy dockets with diminished staff and law clerk support. In Las Vegas at the Justice Court, no new civil cases were accepted for filing for a full week because of lack of personnel to log them in, and there was still a two-hour wait for filing any court papers.[15] In Ohio, a municipal court announced it could no longer accept any civil case filings, on account of the court's having run out of paper and not having money to buy more.[16] In New Hampshire, civil jury trials were eliminated due to a lack of funding. One plaintiff settled a serious personal injury case for $18,500 after learning that the alternative was to wait for more than a year for a trial.[17] In Arizona Common Court, filing fees were raised—in many cases as much as 44 percent—in order to help bridge the funding gap.[18] Positions that were designed to help pro se litigants, such as self-help centers or family court facilitators, are being slashed out of the budgets.

Why should we care? Here is the hard truth: the essential public safety functions of courts are likely to be the last to go, and the civil justice functions the first. When faced with a choice between allowing an alleged criminal to go free because of unconstitutional delays and putting a business dispute on the back burner, courts will choose to sacrifice the business case. Yet, the delays facing civil cases threaten to undermine our system in very real ways.

The World Bank regularly charts courts in developing countries where it is considering making loans. It evaluates the independence of the judiciary—whether judges are beholden to the party rulers for jobs or whether they have ideological and practical independence that allows them to enforce the laws as written. On a more practical level, the World Bank measures dockets, delays, and inconsistencies. It notes that when judiciaries

> carry a large backlog of cases [they] erod[e] individual and property rights, stifl[e] private sector growth, and, in some cases, even violat[e] human rights. Delays affect both the fairness and the efficiency of the judicial system; they impede the public's access to the courts, which, in effect, weakens democracy, the rule of law and the ability to enforce human rights.[19]

In 2010, the Washington Economics Group, Inc., completed a study that documents the impact that delays in the courts have on the Georgia state economy. The report notes that between 2003 and 2008, the caseload went up 24 percent, and in 2009 funding for the courts went down 13 percent.[20] One of the quantifiable impacts is delay in court proceedings, and the authors estimate that

> the combination of the actual reductions in State appropriations for court operations, the actual reductions in fines and fees collected in the past two years, and the added legal costs that parties to civil cases assume due to delays results in an adverse direct economic impact ranging between $155 million to $370 million per annum.[21]

Stephen Zack, president of the American Bar Association, frames Georgia's allocation to the third branch of government in mathematical terms: "How does less than eight-tenths of 1 percent support one third of a whole?"[22] Not surprisingly, the answer is unclear.

The American Bar Association has heard the call. It held a conference in 2009 that focused on the budget crisis in state courts, and Zack has now formed a Task Force on Preservation of the Justice System, cochaired by David Boies and Theodore B. Olson, that is conducting public hearings around the country to document and draw attention to the problem. "This is a crossroad period in civil justice in America," said then New Hampshire chief justice John T. Broderick Jr. at one of those hearings.[23]

There are some silver linings to these clouds. Courts are accepting a level of accountability and public responsiveness that would have seemed discordant a decade ago. There was a time, not too long ago, when any talk of reform or revision met with the bald assertion that there was no staffing to support current operations and certainly the notion of new programs or new approaches was out of the question. Certainly, courts could not be expected to do more (caseload) with less (staff)? That end-run is no longer sufficient. Yes, the public expects the courts to do more with less—and yes, we expect them to do it better, more cost-effectively, and in a way that is more responsive to the needs of the public. Fortunately, more and more courts are doing just that.

The National Center for State Courts and the American Bar Association's joint Justice Is the Business of Government Task Force is developing a set of principles that identify the core functions of state courts as a predicate to establishing a framework for appropriate ongoing funding. The notion is that if we all agree upon the core functions of the court systems and a method of accountability, then the funding process ought to be smoother and more secure. The funding principles that follow on the heels of the core functions focus on demonstrated need, appropriate assessment models, and application of performance measures. In short, courts have to adopt a more businesslike way of doing business and measure themselves in order to justify their budget.

Partially in response to budget realities, and partially just as a result of best-practices thinking, the National Center for State Courts has developed a number of mechanisms through which judges, as well as legislators and the public, can measure court performance. Performance measures called CourTools have been developed for both trial and appellate courts. At the trial court level, such measures include user ratings

on accessibility and fairness, percentage of cases disposed within established time frames, effective use of
jurors, and overall cost of processing a single case (by
case type). For appellate courts, CourTools include
percentage of cases disposed within established time
frames, average cost to the court of resolving a single
case, and surveys of users of the court (appellate lawyers and trial court judges) and court staff. States that
have implemented these performance measures—
Utah and Arizona, for example—are able not only
to track and improve performance, but also to bolster
public trust and confidence by reporting the results of
these measurements to the public at large.

These CourTools measures are but one component
of the National Center for State Courts' High Performance Court Framework. A "performance-based call
to arms,"[24] the framework provides court managers
with insight on how to achieve ongoing, high-quality
administration of justice, focusing on administrative
processes, court culture, and performance measurement
and management. The notion of high-performance
courts is all the more important in today's economic
climate, where ensuring access to the courts is becoming tougher. Courts today are faced with a dire need
"to undertake fundamental changes, such as restruc-
turing delivery systems, redesigning business processes,
expanding the use of technology, and reorganizing
court structure"—what the National Center terms
"reengineering"[25] or "creative innovation."[26] Although
the system faces countless challenges, innovative solutions are out there. And, according to Minnesota state
court judge Kevin Burke, "the most effective court
leaders will challenge their court to face problems for
which there are no simple painless solutions."[27]

Frank Broccolina, former state court administrator in Maryland, writes about seven specific suggestions for the "beleaguered but visionary court leader," which include having court staff trained in how to provide limited advice to litigants about the process, rather than turning them away with the mantra "clerks cannot provide legal advice."[28] He suggests that judges need to take more responsibility for assuring that litigants understand the orders being entered in their cases so that they neither violate them nor return to court for additional guidance.

There are judges around the country who are visionary leaders in their courtrooms and in the system. Oregon's Judge Henry Kantor is an example: "Even with extremely limited resources—still, a judge can make a difference by just talking it through with the person involved."[29] In Colorado state court, Judge Lael Montgomery is acutely aware that people in her courtroom can tell the difference between being "talked 'at' and talked 'to.'"[30] It is with sensitivity to the needs of the litigants—or "mindfulness," as she would say—that Judge Montgomery conducts business in her court.[31]

Visionary court leaders are also walking within the ranks of court administrators. Marcus Reinkensmeyer, court administrator for the judicial branch of Arizona in Maricopa County (Phoenix), has embraced cutting-edge constituent service for the courts. You can hear his commitment in the way his pride does not slip into complacency. "For litigants, we don't want to just hand out forms for them to fill out. We should have videos in the lobby, teaching and helping folks navigate the system. I think we're only about 10 percent of the way there."[32]

In his jurisdiction, Reinkensmeyer strives to balance "high-tech" with "high-touch," relying on collaboration by the bench and bar to make public access a priority. What about a court concierge? "Our court security help with greeting and navigating," he says.[33] "The same thing with phone systems—how many calls does it take to find the next step in the process, from a customer standpoint? The system might work okay for attorneys or 'frequent fliers' in the court, but less so for first-time visitors, whether in family court, traffic, or small claims."[34] These efforts continue, despite that court system having lost approximately 420 positions and $20 million in funding during the last couple of years.[35]

As for the political side, Melinda Taylor, district administrator for the 17th Judicial District in Colorado (operating at less than 85 percent of staffing as of early 2011), suggests that even disasters can lead to progress. She recalls a security machinery breakdown in Adams County, Colorado, and lines around the block for folks to enter the courthouse—all of which was photographed and sent to county commissioners who reacted by appropriating greater resources. "Our current economic difficulties," said Taylor, "actually create an opportunity to be realistically creative and, by the way, hopefully educate the public at the same time."[36]

Viewing her state judicial branch as a trailblazer, Minnesota State court administrator Sue Dosal describes Minnesota citizens as "customers." Having lost 10 percent of court staff statewide, Dosal is finding ways to redesign and innovate service delivery in her courts to move "beyond efficiency to effectiveness."[37] Now, more than ever, relates Dosal, "public trust is what we live and die by."[38] Her perspective in this regard is an important one: "It helps to look at the AOD [Alcohol and Other Drug] court through the addict's eyes or look at the family court though a child's eyes—not for what the parent needs or the system needs, but what is going to yield the very best outcome for that child. That's our lens."[39]

At a time of fiscal crisis, in other words, transparency and accountability can constitute enlightened self-interest—as well as just good government. In order to get adequate funding, courts need to demonstrate both.

As the National Center for State Courts' experts note,

> part of the limitation of technological solutions is that they have been tried without sufficient attention to existing processes and work culture. "Don't pave the cow paths!" is wise counsel against simply automating without first considering whether and how existing processes and workflow should be redesigned.[40]

We have a choice: we can allow the civil justice system to bear the brunt of funding cuts and, as former chief justice Broderick says, "become irrelevant." Or, we can rebuild it. If we are going to rebuild justice, we have to be willing to pay the construction and ongoing maintenance costs, but we have every right to demand accountability, efficiency, and responsiveness in return for those dollars.

So, beyond adequate funding and performance measures for courts, where do we begin the rebuilding?

5

Discovery: The Deluge

University of Michigan professor John Reed related the following story in an article on discovery:

> In a high school class some years ago, the teacher described the prehistoric age in which dinosaurs inhabited the earth, and she described them as enormous, powerful lizards that had no match, no need to fear any other form of life. After class, one boy went up to the teacher and said, "You said the dinosaurs were invincible, but there aren't any more dinosaurs. They're all gone. My question is, who killed the dinosaurs?" "Nobody," she answered. "Nobody killed the dinosaurs. The climate changed and they all died."[1]

Reed's point was to offer a solution to the "dinousaur-sized problems of discovery reform."[2] According to Reed, "Each of us has aspired to be a dinosaur killer...but we haven't done it, and we're not going to kill the dinosaurs. We are, however, each one of us, inevitably a part of the climate. We *can* change the climate—and *that's* how you rid the earth of dinosaurs."[3] (Note: we are not saying that the extinction of a species is a good thing, but we all should acknowledge that if the dinosaurs were still here, chances are we would not be.)

In fact, the discovery climate has changed over time, but perhaps not in the right direction. It was originally devised in order to avoid trial by ambush. The plan was that all parties to a lawsuit would walk into the courtroom knowing the contours of the adversary's case and would be prepared to mount an offense or defense accordingly. No surprise documents or witnesses; no blindsiding.

In criminal cases, the exchange of information is simple and works pretty well. The provisions on disclosure and discovery in the Federal Rules of Criminal Procedure (Federal Rules) are contained in one rule (Rule 16), which is one and a half pages long. It identifies what the prosecutor must disclose, what the defendant must disclose, and the penalties for not doing so. What it doesn't say is that liberty is at stake here.

In contrast, the Federal Rules on discovery and disclosure for civil cases encompass eleven rules, which take up approximately fourteen pages. They spell out in excruciating detail exactly what each party can request from the other, the panoply of tools available to uncover that information, the constraints, and, finally, the enforcement mechanisms.

Of course, the fact that the civil rules are nine times longer than the comparable criminal rules is an overly facile comparison, but in survey after survey, lawyers and judges alike attribute much of the cost and delay in civil litigation to discovery and suggest that the process is frequently abused.

Why? What is the problem here? Let's begin by restating the two premises of civil litigation: (1) the plaintiff need only give notice of the nature of the lawsuit at the outset, without details, and (2) discovery is intended to be a broad and deep process by which both parties find out about the case. Just to continue our comparison to criminal cases for a moment, criminal cases do not operate on either premise. The prosecutor must demonstrate probable cause to believe that the offense was committed by the defendant before any further proceedings are allowed. At that point, the prosecutor *must* disclose various facts and documents or risk being thrown out of court and/or disciplined. The defendant's duty to disclose information is much more limited but equally seriously enforced. In criminal cases, discovery is conditional (the prosecutor must demonstrate that there is evidence supporting the charges), clearly defined, and automatic.

In civil cases, discovery is none of those things, and, if you don't ask for exactly the right thing, you might not get it. Remember the main arrows in the discovery quiver:

- Interrogatories
- Requests for admission
- Depositions—of fact witnesses or expert witnesses
- Requests for production of documents

Once the defendant to a lawsuit has answered the plaintiff's complaint, discovery begins. First, both sides are likely to fire off interrogatories, which should be targeted and tailored. Sometimes they are, sometimes they are not. With the advent of the personal computer and word processing in the 1970s, interrogatories grew to pages upon pages of definitions and boilerplate questions—whether or not they were designed to annoy and aggravate, they certainly

did so. As a result, interrogatories are now limited in
many jurisdictions to a certain number of questions.

Requests for admission are a species of interroga-
tory, but as the name suggests, ask the opposing party
to actually admit a fact in controversy. Requests for
admission, too, can be lengthy and potentially abusive.

Depositions are another tool and they, too, can
spin out of control—in number, in length, and, most
certainly, in dollar signs. This can be true for depositions of nonexpert witnesses, but is certainly true for
depositions of expert witnesses. Take, for example,
a thirty-six-day deposition in a California toxic tort
case, attended by more than a dozen attorneys on
each day. Or take a medical malpractice case in which
twelve experts were identified by one side, and counsel
flew all over the country deposing each one of them.
At approximately $1,000 per hour for the expert, plus
the attorneys' fees, the court reporter (stenographer)
costs, and the travel costs, each deposition had better
be good. Instead, depositions are often an opportunity
for one attorney to whipsaw the witness and either
"assess credibility" or run up costs for settlement purposes. In a recent study by the Federal Judicial Center, each expert deposition conducted was associated
with 11 percent higher costs for plaintiffs and each
nonexpert deposition was associated with approximately 5 percent higher costs for both plaintiffs and
defendants.[4] Some experienced lawyers report that
they are often likely to choose not to conduct depositions of expert witnesses because they cost too much
and just serve to alert the other side to weaknesses of
the expert; however, they worry that if they then lose
the case at trial, the client could claim malpractice for
that decision because the rules anticipate depositions

of all experts. Apparently, if it is in the rules, it must be good practice.

Then we come to requests for production of documents and one of the most profound changes on the litigation landscape: e-discovery, the discovery of electronically stored information (ESI). Here, the premise of unlimited discovery mixes with a world of unlimited information and, like two chemical components, creates an explosion.

Jill Griset, a partner in the Charlotte, North Carolina office of the McGuireWoods law firm, recently represented a client who had been sued for copyright infringement. The client owned a business directory that included advertisements with photos that the plaintiff claimed were its property. During discovery, the plaintiff demanded that the publisher produce an inventory listing of every ad that contained a disputed picture.

> Our client had a large database containing millions of advertisements but it was not organized by the source of the photos—it was organized by advertiser. We argued that there was no good way of searching for the ads that may have contained the allegedly infringing photos. We tried to use sophisticated image-recognition software, but because the photos were imbedded in the ads and contained multiple layers of media, the software could not find the photos without taking apart each file manually at a cost of millions of dollars. We argued that we should do a statistical sampling and a manual review, and that if we then found any ads with infringing images, we would then search for all ads of those advertisers. We then proposed

coming up with a damage calculation based on
that statistical sampling. The plaintiff repeat-
edly rejected our request for a sampling and kept
insisting that we search all of our files, which we
kept arguing was virtually impossible or would be
extremely expensive and take years to do.[5]

The judge was not sympathetic. "Once we started
producing documents, the plaintiff backed off," Griset
said, "and the case was soon resolved. But it's a good
example of the problems that occur when the opposing party and the court don't understand the producing party's systems or the technology."[6]

Nor can Griset's tale be ascribed to any technopho-
bia on her part. She is, in fact, among her profession's
leading practitioners of data-driven litigation. Rare
within her profession, Griset is fluent in gigabytes and
terabytes, native files and TIFF files, legacy data and
metadata. These are the building blocks of the search for
the truth in much of twenty-first-century litigation—at
least for those who know how to use them.

A few weeks before recounting the near-paralysis
by e-discovery, Griset was standing in a nondescript
office park a few miles south of her office. The room
is large enough to hold an entire floor of a typical
suburban house. Ringing the walls is a bank of some
fifty computer stations, bisected by another line of
PCs that stretch from the back wall toward the front
door. On any given day, the room is packed with contract attorneys hired on a temporary basis by Griset to
hunch over the glowing rectangles and review document after document. A low thrum occasionally will
infuse the place, as the searchers lean over to compare
screenshots. But for the most part, the soundtrack

consists of the soft clicks of a few hundred fingertips on a few dozen keyboards.

This is the heart of the modern-day lawsuit machine. Behind most complex commercial litigation, and increasingly even within the more intimate confines of divorce court, temporary workers are cyclically assembled to search for needles in a world of virtual haystacks. It is a revolution, of sorts, and it is not being televised.

The lion's share of the search for documents used to occur in office basements, warehouses, and regulatory agency libraries. Now it happens in legal war rooms such as Griset's, where ESI is vetted through the keyboard. The amount of time spent trying to find evidence once depended on whether a document could actually be found, say, on a shelf or in a drawer. The brave new world of electronic discovery, however, presents an evidentiary landscape that is potentially never-ending. An infinite universe of discoverable information is on the horizon.

Griset explained:

> In the old paper world, defendants often did not go to the trouble of throwing out some box of documents. So it was a simple matter of tracking that down and going through the contents. But in an electronic world, you have e-mail and document deletion policies in place. On rare occasions, that means stuff is gone for good, but usually it means that it's just gone somewhere harder to find.[7]

Ultimately, e-discovery might allow attorneys to target discovery with efficiency and find documents on point without warehouse review (if the parameters are circumscribed by the rules or the presiding judge). But for the time being, the e-discovery morass is about volume and cost, confusion and fear. Let's begin with volume. Consider that more than 99 percent of the world's information is now generated electronically— approximately 100 billion e-mails and 5 billion instant messages are generated every day.[8] One study suggests that the volume of electronic information increases at an annual rate of 30 percent.[9]

As the world of ESI grows, so does the world of ESI that has the potential to be unearthed in a lawsuit. Now add into the equation of unlimited discovery the component of almost limitless information. E-mails, text messages, instant messages, voice mails, websites, call logs, word processing documents, and digital photos are now among the information that must be made available during the discovery process. Absent from this list are the backup, archived, or deleted versions of the above information that live in our cell phones and computers long after we think they have been deleted. With all of this information now at issue in civil litigation, costs have skyrocketed. Writing in *Corporate Counsel*, Alan Cohen estimated that as recently as 2002, a "midsize case" typically involved five gigabytes of data, or the rough equivalent of 500,000 pages of printed e-mails without attachments.[10] That, by the way, is the equivalent of 1,000 books on a Kindle. Also consider that this estimate was made five years before the introduction of the first iPhone and seven years before Google's operating system for smartphones burst onto the scene. Cohen, however, notes that as of 2007, the year in which his *Corporate Counsel* article was published, "anything less than 500 GB is considered small."[11] In a December

2007 survey, attorneys in some of the largest law firms and corporations in the United States and Canada chose electronic discovery—ahead of globalization—as the issue sure to "have the biggest impact on the practice of law in the next five years."[12] Majorities of respondents to a 2010 IAALS survey of chief legal officers and general counsel reported that the cost of pretrial litigation for a typical company has increased, and that the total overall yearly cost of pretrial litigation has increased.[13] Respondents reporting the latter commonly cited discovery in general—e-discovery in particular—as the basis for the trend.[14] One respondent noted that

> the discovery of electronic data is clearly the most important new litigation concern to arise in the past few decades. The costs of compliance (preservation, review, production) are enormous; the amount of data is massive; the ignorance of effective retrieval systems is rampant; the knowledge of the courts is limited; and, the rules of procedure are still antiquated.[15]

The cost of e-discovery in civil litigation has many causes and accumulates at almost every stage of the process. One of the most problematic and costly aspects of e-discovery involves the retention and preservation of ESI. Litigation is won and lost on evidence—it is the foundation of the justice system. When claims arise, parties immediately turn their attention to the evidence that supports their position, which is often in the possession of an opponent. This is the situation the discovery process is designed to address, and, as a corollary to this process, parties have an affirmative duty to preserve evidence that is even potentially relevant to a lawsuit and to do so as soon as a lawsuit is anticipated. This duty to preserve evidence becomes very complicated when dealing with ESI. As many of us know, technology has a mind of its own. Unbeknownst to us, computers and other electronics routinely alter and delete files and records. The point at which a party's duty to preserve is triggered is often unclear, and, as 2011 American College President Gregory Joseph points out, "uncertainty is expensive."[16] On one hand, because computers routinely destroy information to make room for new information, preserving electronically stored evidence creates expensive storage issues. Furthermore, where preservation begins too late, parties can be seriously sanctioned for destroying evidence. The pervasive lack of understanding of e-discovery exacerbates these issues.

Once the ESI has been preserved, it then has to be located, which can be more problematic than you would think. In the age of paper-only discovery, most organizations filed documents according to filing systems understood both within the organization and by the legal professionals brought in when a lawsuit hit. Using these systems, clients were more likely to know where relevant information was stored and how to access it easily. Today, most organizations have not organized their ESI in a way that facilitates a quick and easy review of relevant information—both because of an overall lack of preparation for litigation (discussed below) and also because of the very nature of ESI: multiple formats, versions, and locations. Deleting an e-mail from Outlook, moving a Word document to the recycle bin, or deleting a text message does not permanently delete the file. It resides in a technological netherworld on our computers and smartphones, and the journey over the river Styx to uncover it can be costly.

Assuming it can be located, the ESI has to be reviewed—probably more than once—in order to determine whether it is relevant to the lawsuit in the first instance and then to determine whether the information contains privileged content. The Rand Corporation has reported that as much as 75–90 percent of the costs of e-discovery are attributable to "eyes-on" review by attorneys of ESI.[17] In a forthcoming Rand survey of a handful of Fortune 250 corporations, preliminary results suggest that this process of reviewing e-discovery for relevancy and privilege consumed a significant amount of the total expenditures undertaken during the discovery process. Furthermore, outside counsel fees incurred for the purpose of this review can be significant. Lastly, the ESI determined to be relevant and nonprivileged must be organized and produced to the opposing side, and then reviewed by them.

The skyrocketing and disproportionate costs of all of this can be heart-stopping. Verizon has collected data on the costs of e-discovery and internally benchmarked the costs of processing, reviewing, culling, and producing one gigabyte of data at between $5,000 and $7,000 (assuming the use of precise keyword searches).[18] If a "midsize" case produces five hundred gigabytes of data, this means affected organizations should expect to spend $2.5 to $3.5 million on the review and production of ESI.[19] And the continued explosion of information might well mean that discovery will only get bigger and more expensive. A 2008 report by the Rand Institute for Civil Justice warned that even in low-value cases, the costs of e-discovery "could dominate the underlying stakes in dispute."[20]

The increased use of "e-discovery vendors" to handle this process—in response to increasing costs of performing these processes in-house—is also generating costs. E-discovery vendors can run between $125 and $600 per hour for clicking through electronic documents.[21] A number of years ago, Robert Krebs, a litigation paralegal, worked on a smaller case in which just a fraction of the data the plaintiff requested was located on seventy-five hard drives. The processing quotes for just twenty of those hard drives ranged from $400,000 to nearly $600,000, a price that included no attorney hours.[22] The low estimate of liability in that case was about $750,000, and the "pie-in-the-sky estimate was about $6 million."[23]

Also contributing to the problem are confusion and a culture of fear. Big law firms, big corporations, and some judges are increasingly sophisticated about e-discovery, but they are the exception, not the rule. One judge, when asked in 2009 if a case involving e-discovery had come before his court, did not even know what e-discovery was. He thought it was the same thing as e-filing, a process by which the parties file documents electronically with the court. While speaking about his court's new electronic case management system, California Supreme Court Justice Ming Chin received the following question from one of the lawyers in attendance: "In order to access this, do I have to have a computer?"[24] "So," said Justice Chin, "we have a lot of educating to do."[25] Many judges have neither the inclination nor the technological background even to begin to understand the problems. A 2008 Rand study reported that technology continues to evolve faster than the law,[26] and the danger is "that outmoded and ineffective discovery paradigms could be inappropriately applied by sitting judges, thereby leading to inefficiencies and potential inequities."[27]

Attorneys may not be much better. E-discovery expert Craig Ball argues that the majority of lawyers (even big-firm lawyers) "are unsophisticated about ESI and e-discovery."[28] Studies released by various e-discovery consultants in 2007 demonstrated extraordinary levels of unpreparedness: anywhere from 65 percent to 94 percent of the organizations responding indicated that they were not ready.[29] The findings of the IAALS chief litigation officer and general counsel survey illustrate significant resource gaps with respect to e-discovery. A strong minority (40 percent) of respondents indicated a belief that their company does not have the ability and/or infrastructure to implement "an adequate but targeted [litigation] hold without undue cost or delay."[30] Furthermore, 65 percent of respondents indicated their company does not have sufficient in-house or outside expertise and infrastructure to conduct an e-discovery search "without undue cost and delay."[31]

The word one respondent used to describe how his or her company deals with e-discovery? *Luck.* It rang true to legal observers in 2009 when the American College of Trial Lawyers characterized e-discovery as "a nightmare" and "a morass."[32] An International Legal Technology Association purchasing survey found that law firm information technology managers throughout the country listed "attorney education" as one of their biggest e-discovery challenges.[33]

It's no surprise, really. The culture and profession of law has long viewed itself as more of an art than a

science. E-discovery is largely mechanical. It's technical. And for a profession schooled in the presumption
of protecting precedent (*stare decisis*) and more generally predisposed toward slow, incremental change,
e-discovery is viewed (somewhat oxymoronically) as
both menial and intimidating. Lawyers have become
both too comfortable and reflexively aggressive in discovery, regularly submitting requests that seek "any
and all" documents pertaining to a particular subject.
Bad as that could be in a pen-and-paper era, any and
all requests become positively oppressive with e-discovery, for both the seeking and the producing parties.

Judges don't get it, CFOs don't get it, and lawyers don't get it. IT directors get it, but they might
have received little or no guidance from, say, the general counsel on how he or she might need to access
the data. The most powerful flashlight in the world
is of marginal utility in an unlit warehouse that has
been randomly stuffed to the rafters over the course
of many years.

In 2001, the e-discovery reality caused tremors
across the United States when multinational financial
giant UBS Warburg was hit with a $29 million judg-
ment in a sexual discrimination suit brought by an
investment banker named Laura Zubulake. A major
factor contributing to the ruling was UBS Warburg's
mismanagement of electronic data: in defiance of
court orders, the employer had lost or destroyed vast
quantities of e-mails relating to the suit. With subsequent rulings, the so-called *Zubulake* decisions established guidelines increasingly cited by other courts
that impose electronic information preservation and
retrieval rules on litigants, along with potentially
devastating financial sanctions on those who fail to

comply.[34] In the wake of her rulings on these questions, US District Judge Shira Scheindlin expressed hope that a newly efficient and less costly litigation process would emerge.

In December 2006, influenced by pioneering work from The Sedona Conference, several e-discovery-related amendments to the Federal Rules became effective. They were designed to help parties address the problems that e-discovery poses. These amendments include the following:

- The requirement that the parties meet and confer specifically on e-discovery issues early in the litigation
- A discovery exemption created for ESI that is not "reasonably accessible because of undue burden or cost"
- The ability of the court to shift the cost of producing ESI under certain circumstances to the party requesting the information[35]

Has the rule and the evolving case law worked to smooth out the problems? So far, it appears not.

In 2010, with *The Pension Committee of the University of Montreal Pension Plan v. Banc of America Securities*, Judge Scheindlin herself (in an opinion subtitled "*Zubulake* Revisited: Six Years Later") expressed frustration at ignorant and indifferent lawyers who have failed to heed the courts on e-discovery.[36] She imposed sanctions and leveled a withering critique on attorneys in the case for failure to abide by discovery standards.

There are innovative courts around the country starting to cope with the e-discovery dilemma in some very hands-on ways. For example, certain courtrooms in the Seventh Circuit—under the leadership of Chief District Judge James Holderman and Magistrate Judge Nan Nolan—put into effect in October 2009 a pilot project designed to ensure early and informal exchange of information on commonly encountered issues relating to evidence preservation and discovery. The project is gaining steam and, so far, demonstrating that when judges and attorneys work together, they can both save clients money and streamline the resolution of issues.

The dual reality of the system is that discovery of electronic information can, indeed, enhance the search for the truth. Both because we all run at the mouth (virtually speaking) far more than ever before, and because all of those perhaps-ill-advised comments are discoverable, there is an argument that e-discovery is quite simply a good thing because it will uncover more needles in more haystacks than ever before. But, the other reality is that even with cooperative attorneys and attentive judges, it is expensive. It increases the dollars required to be invested in litigation. If expanded discovery was multiplying the costs of the system, e-discovery operates in exponents. Even if e-discovery permits the uncovering of the truth in some cases, it most certainly causes injustice in others by exorbitant transaction costs, cases that are leveraged into inappropriate settlements, and cases that can never be filed. Truth in some cases has a heavy cost in others. Many lawyers suggest that the 80-20 rule applies here as well: 20 percent of the discovery yields 80 percent of the information, and the remaining 20 percent of the information consumes 80 percent of the cost. Even understanding that the 20 percent may, in some cases, be dispositive, we might need to settle for the 80 percent if, in the wide majority of the cases, the diminished costs in fact increase access and just outcomes.

Rather than addressing the symptoms (rearranging the deck chairs on the *Titanic*) and revising or refining e-discovery, we urge reconsideration of the underlying cause. Let's return for a moment to discovery in criminal cases—conditional, confined, and automatic. Those premises can and should be made to operate in civil cases by changing the rules of procedure.

6

The Conestoga Wagon on the Information Highway

Judge John Kane of the federal district court in Colorado calls the civil justice system a "Conestoga wagon on the information highway," a canvas-topped relic bumping along in the Ethernet. The chassis of this wagon is a group of rules of civil procedure that were adopted three-quarters of a century ago: the Federal Rules of Civil Procedure (Federal Rules), which control procedure in federal courts across the nation and which are mirrored in most state courts in whole or in part. Part of the rebuilding process must include the reworking of those rules. Just as the Conestoga wagons started their westward trek laden with every conceivable packable item—and left trails of pianos, china chests, and clothing in their wake—so, too, is our insistence upon a heavily laden litigation system leaving detritus. Only, in our instance, it involves real people and real claims.

In the law, in the courtroom, and to every single litigant, the rules of procedure governing civil lawsuits are terribly, terribly important. Although Congress and state legislatures write the laws, these rules of civil procedure are generally the province of the courts.

For example, the Federal Rules are the work product, initially, of lawyers, judges, and academics serving on committees of the Judicial Conference of the United States—a twenty-seven-judge body chaired by the chief justice of the United States—which oversees the administration of the federal judicial system. The rules committees (one for criminal rules, one for civil rules, and several others) develop proposed amendments through hearings and research and recommend changes to the Judicial Conference, which may then refer them to the Supreme Court. The Court in turn can consider whether to transmit the proposed rules to Congress. Once it receives the proposed rules, Congress has several months to act on them. If it does nothing, the proposed rules go into effect and have the force of law. The state courts have some version of a similar plan whereby the courts themselves have primary, if not exclusive, control over the rules. In some states, the legislature has a role; in others, it does not.

When they were adopted in 1938, the Federal Rules were state-of-the-art. At the time, people were driving Packards, did not have the option to fly by jet planes, had no computers or cell phones, and went to trial with one file tucked under an arm. The Federal Rules were, indeed, an innovation in their day. In the early twentieth century, before the "new" rules, American civil procedure was confusing at best, chaotic at worst. Each federal district had its own rules, and there was frequently little overlap among procedures from district to district. Procedure in many states was further complicated by the rigid and formalistic requirements of the then ubiquitous Field Code, which required that claims be stated by using only certain words or phrases. All of this complexity led to very formalistic requirements that were traps for the unwary.

Hence, there was a dire need for simple, uniform rules of federal civil procedure. During the same 1906 speech to the American Bar Association in which he lamented the election of judges, Roscoe Pound issued the century's first major call for procedural reform—though not recognized as such at the time it was given.[1] He planted the seeds for reform, which then took thirty years to bear fruit.

While it was never anticipated that every procedure available in the Federal Rules would apply to every case, the gist of the new procedural scheme was relatively straightforward:

- The plaintiff would initiate the case with a short and plain statement sufficient to put the defendant on notice of the nature of the claim (called notice pleading), and the defendant would reply with an answer, responding to the assertions set forth by the plaintiff.

- The parties would then engage in discovery to collect information relevant to the claims and defenses before trial and thus avoid any surprises once trial began.

- Various discovery mechanisms, pieces of which were then in place in state courts around the nation, were all corralled and placed into the Federal Rules. Such mechanisms included interrogatories (formal questions posed to the other side); requests for production of documents; requests for entering onto land or physical inspection; request for mental or physical examination; depositions (out of court questioning of a prospective witness under oath by the attorney for the other side); and request for admissions.

The discovery mechanisms were the real heart of the plan, designed to be broad and deep so as to serve the search for the truth. Nonetheless, they were never supposed to become the purpose of the litigation. They were a means to an end—tools to be used in avoiding trial by ambush in the courtroom. They were, ironically, designed to avoid gamesmanship, create an even playing field, and tee up the case for a just outcome before a judge or jury. The rules of discovery were never intended to become an end in themselves. Over time, the tail has most definitely begun to wag the dog—but we are getting ahead of ourselves.

The rules were, by most measures, a good fit for the civil litigation climate of the 1940s and 1950s. Transcontinental travel was a rare luxury, and discovery was necessarily limited in this precomputer, prephotocopier, pre-e-mail era. Major categories of substantive litigation that have driven the past thirty years of American legal life—such as class actions, mass tort litigation, and civil rights litigation—had not yet appeared in any significant volume. Under these conditions, and especially in comparison to the complicated system that preceded it, the new procedures were largely embraced by the legal community. Indeed, many words have been invoked to describe the first decades following the birth of the Federal Rules, all emphasizing the position and prestige afforded the rules and the rulemaking process through which they were conceived—*a triumph, influential, transformative.* University of California professor Stephen C. Yeazell writes that "for several decades after the Rules' adoption, one might have thought that they had inaugurated procedural perfection."[2]

It was during this period that the federal rulemaking process and the rules themselves were copied widely at the state level. Even in those states where procedural rules did not mirror their federal counterparts, the effects of the rules were nonetheless felt. In short, according to Professor Robert Bone, a leading civil procedure scholar, this was a "golden age of court rulemaking."[3]

Exactly when this golden age ended is difficult to pin down, but the general consensus is that by their fortieth anniversary in 1978, the gold was tarnishing. As early as 1968, studies were exploring the relationship between discovery practices and cost increases in civil litigation. Influenced by a study dispelling the notion that discovery was causing an increase in costs, in 1970 the Judicial Conference developed amendments to the rules that further expanded discovery. The 1970 amendments are widely considered to be the high point of party-controlled discovery in the United States. The rejection of a connection between discovery and litigation costs, however, would not last long. The 1970s saw the real advent of the information age—personal computers and word processors changed not only the practice of law, but the related practice of discovery—and the inexorable acceptance of the fact that discovery increases costs of litigation.

The volume of available information held by parties to lawsuits began to expand, and simultaneously, courts around the country were issuing opinions interpreting the rules to permit a broad swath of discovery through that information and even endorsing "fishing expeditions," a term that applies to the practice of demanding very broad discovery in order to fish through it and find the relevant pieces. In a 1947 case cited by courts around the country for decades, the US Supreme Court decision held:

We agree, of course, that the deposition-discovery
rules are to be accorded a broad and liberal treatment. No longer can the time-honored cry of
"fishing expedition" serve to preclude a party from
inquiring into the facts underlying his opponent's
case. Mutual knowledge of all the relevant facts
gathered by both parties is essential to proper litigation. To that end, either party may compel the other
to disgorge whatever facts he has in his possession.[4]

To be sure, there are legal and social commentators who point to that evolution as serving the
interests of truth-seeking—the uncovering of smok-
ing guns and needles in haystacks in some renowned
cases. Others look at litigation practices from before
and after this evolution as evidence that the interests
of truth-seeking were sufficiently served prior to the
introduction of the expansive discovery system. In a
2010 presentation to attorneys and judges, Washington, DC attorney Mark Hansen examined the "trials without discovery" of the past and the "discovery
without trials" of the present.[5] Hansen chronicled
influential cases of the past in which skilled lawyers
such as Abraham Lincoln operated without discovery, instead employing ingenuity to present cases to
juries. Hansen compared these cases to more recent
cases defined by excessive and expensive discovery
with no jury catharsis, but rather a complex settlement. For example, in an early 1980s case between
the US government and IBM, 2,500 depositions were
taken and 66 million pages of documents assembled.
Time joked: "What has digested 50 million pieces
of paper, chewed on 500 witnesses and has 38 legs?
Answer: the rival teams of lawyers appearing in court

to argue the Government's mammoth IBM antitrust suit."[6] After all this, the case was dropped before trial.

Whether one is a discovery proponent or opponent or something in between, the unavoidable truth is that the combination of burgeoning information and limitless discovery began to point the system in an unfortunate direction: skyrocketing costs, overdiscovery, and discovery abuse. The history of rules amendments since 1970 is largely a history of trying to put the discovery genie back in the bottle, first through an emphasis on judicial case management and then through tinkering with discovery provisions.

The first proposed solution was expanded judicial case management. Increased attention to judicial management began in earnest with a series of Federal Judicial Center studies in the late 1970s finding that the use of court management techniques could help keep discovery under control and decrease time to resolution for a case.[7] Accordingly, amendments to the rules in 1980 provided for increased judicial control over discovery practices by mandating discovery conferences, and in 1983 the Federal Rules were amended to make case management an express goal of pretrial procedure by mandating a scheduling order to enable the judge to manage the entire pretrial phase effectively. During this time, case management principles couched as "delay reduction" techniques swept through the courts, and judges were trained in case management techniques. Reformers focused on "time to disposition" in the case (measuring the time from filing to final resolution) as the end-all-and-be-all. This was paired with a new capacity for courts to produce reports about such things as open cases and average time to disposition. What happened was predictable. Judges began to manage toward a goal of decreasing the time from the filing of the case to ultimate outcome. They encouraged settlements, because that accelerated disposition and gave them back some docket time. But this sometimes involved so-called cram-down settlements, leaving many parties feeling railroaded.

This was not occurring in a vacuum. It all transpired in a climate in which attorneys historically had sole control of their cases, particularly in the state systems, and to a somewhat lesser extent in the federal system. Prior to the case management trend, when the attorneys in a case were ready for trial, they submitted a "notice of setting," and that triggered action from the court. Judges during that time typically had no involvement in "managing" the case in the pretrial phase—it rested entirely with the attorneys. In the late 1980s and early 1990s, the expectations began to change, and there was an increased focus on the appropriate role of the judge in the pretrial preparation of a case. Perhaps the judge should manage the case, monitor the timeline, and pay attention to the particular needs of the case. In the 1990 Civil Justice Reform Act, Congress mandated specific case management techniques in ten pilot districts. These included differential treatment, early and ongoing control of the pretrial process, and judicial involvement in the discovery process. While the effectiveness of many Civil Justice Reform Act provisions was questionable, those relating to early case management showed the most promise for reducing time to disposition.

In 1993, new amendments to the Federal Rules granted the courts more control over the discovery process and other pretrial matters by emphasizing that a major objective of the pretrial conference should be to establish appropriate controls on the extent and timing of discovery. These amendments also encouraged the court to include, in the scheduling order, a timeline relating to initial disclosures. Also in 1993, and on the heels of the case management revolution, rules amendments limited the numbers of depositions and interrogatories and required parties to automatically disclose certain information relevant to the case without waiting for a discovery request. These latter provisions were introduced in optional format in 1993 and made mandatory in every federal district court in 2000. These amendments require parties to disclose witnesses and documents that the disclosing party might use to support its claims or defenses. Also at this time, the scope of discovery was narrowed from information relevant to the subject matter of the action to information that was relevant to the claims and defenses of the parties. Throughout these amendments, some states found their own ways of trying to address the information explosion that was happening in federal courts, though many more states just kept pace with the Federal Rules, mirroring changes step for step.

As if the existing discovery problems were not bad enough, enter the gigabytes. Over the past decade, the parabolic growth of electronically stored information has presented new problems of cost and delay. As discussed in the prior chapter, in a growing number of cases, the cost of restoring, reviewing, and producing relevant ESI might be in the millions of dollars. Amendments to the rules in 2006 sought to address some of the issues raised specifically by electronic discovery, but deep concerns about the Federal Rules' ability to keep up with the rapid march of technology remain.

The general public has been disenchanted with the civil justice system for some time now. For example, in a 2005 Harris Poll, 54 percent of those surveyed did not trust the legal system to defend them against a baseless claim, and 56 percent suggested that fundamental changes are needed.[8] Now, lawyers and judges themselves are chiming in, bemoaning the gamesmanship in the system, the delays, *and* the costs. They worry that access to the system is increasingly difficult, not just for the indigent, but also for the middle class.

A wealth of surveys and studies undertaken in the last few years illustrate the disenchantment felt among lawyers and judges. In addition to a survey of the American College of Trial Lawyers (ACTL) undertaken by IAALS and the American College Task Force, these surveys include the American Bar Association (ABA) Section of Litigation and the National Employment Lawyers Association (NELA), which have surveyed their respective memberships about their perceptions of the civil justice system. IAALS has conducted surveys of the Arizona and Oregon bench and bar, and chief legal officers and general counsel nationwide, and—in concert with the Searle Center at Northwestern University—state and federal trial judges.

Additionally, empirical studies of court dockets published by IAALS and by the Federal Judicial Center examine the underlying causes of delay in civil case processing. What contributes to delay? Which causes lie outside the docket? To what extent can judges, attorneys, and court administrators adopt new procedures to address such lags? In 2008, IAALS released a study with data drawn from nearly 7,700 federal civil cases that had terminated between October 1, 2005, and September 30, 2006, in eight federal courts across the country. More recently, the Federal Judicial Center completed a national closed-case study and survey of attorneys in May and June 2009 to examine cost and delay in federal courts.

What do all of these data show us? A very strong consensus emerges from the surveys that the cost of civil justice is too high. In all surveys in which the question was asked, at least three out of four respondents indicated that litigation generally is too expensive.[9] A respondent to the IAALS chief legal officer and general counsel survey explained how complicity often rests with all of the professionals involved:

> The plaintiff[s'] lawyers take the tactic of suing as many defendants as possible under as many legal theories as possible to "see what sticks"... The defense attorneys, billing at an hourly rate, benefit [from the resulting] broad discovery and the amount of time and effort it requires...The judges...often do not grant motions...that could serve to whittle the complaint down to the true cause of actions [or] act to sufficiently limit discovery. By freely granting motions to continue, they allow the cases to drag on for years.[10]

The surveys also shed light on some of the unfortunate consequences of the excessive expense. Lawyers across the country turn away clients based on the dollar value of the case. More than 80 percent of the respondents to the American College, American Bar Association, and National Employment Lawyers Association surveys indicated that their law firms turn down cases when it is not cost-effective to take them.[11] The most common threshold given for turning down a case was $100,000 (a case in which at least $100,000 in damages is at issue), a considerable amount of money for most of us.[12] Similarly, the surveys show a strong consensus that some cases are settled primarily because of the cost of continuing to litigate through the court process. In the American College and American Bar Association surveys, more than 80 percent of all respondents indicated that costs force cases to settle that, based on the merits, should not settle.[13] At least 70 percent of attorney respondents to the American College, American Bar Association, and National Employment Lawyers Association surveys expressed agreement with the statement that "discovery is too expensive."[14]

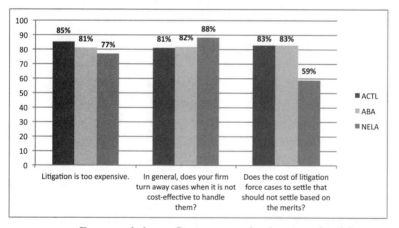

Excess and Access: Consensus on the American Civil Justice Landscape (Gerety 2011).

Cost is not the only factor at work here; significant delay is also a problem. In 2007, the percentage of civil cases more than three years old was 6.6 percent—in 2010, it was 15.8 percent of all cases.[15] Of the cases included in the 2008 IAALS study of federal litigation, roughly one-third took more than one year to resolve.[16] More and more cases are languishing. Too many of America's courtrooms will come to resemble a freeway in gridlock—an artery designed for fluid transportation that more often approximates a parking lot. An incident or accident that might take seconds to unfold on the street or in a boardroom can take years to be examined and debated in a courtroom.

Delays in civil litigation are not only frustrating, they cost money. More than 90 percent of the American College Fellow respondents, 82 percent of the American Bar Association respondents, 79 percent of the general counsel respondents, and 73 percent of the National Employment Lawyers Association respondents indicated that delays in litigation run up the costs.[17] The Federal Judicial Center analysis supports this, finding that every 1 percent increase in case duration is associated with a 0.32 percent increase in costs for plaintiffs and a 0.26 percent increase in costs for defendants.[18] Time means money. Furthermore, in the American College, American Bar Association, and National Employment Lawyers Association surveys, the "time required to complete discovery" was identified over any other single cause as the primary cause of delay.[19] Over 80 percent of respondents to the IAALS and Searle Center survey of judges identified the time required to complete discovery as a significant cause of delay—ranking highest of all options given.[20]

During the delay, litigants can feel economic pressure to settle the case even when they believe they would prevail on the merits. If they do not settle, they have to contend with increasingly fading memories, then wait longer still for financial resolution and emotional closure. And lengthy cases affect more than the litigants. From the judge's perspective, cases that linger on the docket squander time and resources that could be spent on other matters, and they often require redundant efforts as turnover occurs among the ranks of judicial officers. For attorneys, long cases similarly devour resources (albeit at frequently high rates of pay) and cause client-attorney dissatisfaction. And for the general public, extended cases epitomize governmental inefficiency, eroding confidence in the judicial system.

Furthermore, the 2008 IAALS docket study found that the *same type* of case can take an average of *two or three times longer* to resolve in one federal district court than in another.[21]

CIVIL RIGHTS—EMPLOYMENT CASES

District	Number of Cases	Mean Time in Days
District of Idaho	35	507.03
Western District of Wisconsin	31	257.16

INSURANCE CASES

District	Number of Cases	Mean Time in Days
District of Idaho	19	433.63
Western District of Wisconsin	15	133.93

OTHER CIVIL RIGHTS CASES

District	Number of Cases	Mean Time in Days
District of Colorado	192	423.61
Eastern District of Missouri	169	250.42

OTHER CONTRACT CASES

District	Number of Cases	Mean Time in Days
District of Delaware	48	450.08
Western District of Wisconsin	55	148.56

As a practical matter, this means that litigants can wait months or even years longer for a resolution to their dispute, simply because the case was filed in one court rather than another. This sends a pernicious, even decivilizing, message to the public: justice is relative. The other message from that research is that delay is not inevitable; it can be managed and reduced.

These problems are compounded by the sharp increase in the number of self-represented litigants, particularly in the state court systems, but in the federal courts as well. More than 4 million users of the California court system were self-represented in 2003.[22] In the same year, one of the parties to a lawsuit was self-represented in 85 percent of all civil cases in New Hampshire District Court and 48 percent of all civil cases in New Hampshire Superior Court.[23] In a 2009 study of judges throughout the United States undertaken by the American Bar Association Coalition for Justice, 60 percent of judges stated that fewer parties were being represented.[24] The survey also found consensus that the court is negatively impacted by parties not well represented (78 percent) and the self-represented party's case is negatively impacted (62 percent).[25]

While still on the New Hampshire Supreme Court, Justice John Broderick Jr. found "the rising number of self-represented litigants" to be the "single biggest challenge confronting the state courts in America."[26] Furthermore, the face of self-represented litigants is changing, according to Justice Broderick: "Their ranks now include more members of the middle-class and a rising number of small businesses."[27] According to Justice Broderick, "the simple truth is that more and more parties are coming to court alone at the same time more and more lawyers are becoming too expensive."[28]

There is another factor at work, one that we do not address in this book but that requires a reference:

attorneys' fees. The hourly rate is a much-maligned way of delivering legal services. It is perceived as disconnecting the interests of the lawyer from the interests of the client, because inefficiency, overlawyering, and duplication of effort can be rewarded under an hourly fee structure. Whether or not that is true, there is a movement afoot in the country to find ways to bill attorney services other than by an hourly rate. For example, the Association of Corporate Counsel (ACC), an association of in-house counsel, has adopted what it terms the ACC Value Challenge. It has launched an initiative to reconnect value and costs for legal services, which will, among other things, "develop methodologies and metrics that corporate counsel can use to assess the strengths and weaknesses of law firm vendors" and "create tools that in-house counsel and firms can share to drive change in the performance of value-based legal services."[29] The project proposes a covenant between in-house counsel and outside counsel that includes a promise to offer value-based fee alternatives, such as fixed-fee services. The underlying premise is that

> many traditional law firm business models and many of the approaches to lawyer training and cost management are not aligned with what corporate clients want and need: value-driven, high-quality legal services that deliver solutions for a reasonable cost and develop lawyers as counselors (not just content-providers), advocates (not just process-doers) and professional partners.[30]

Sounds a bit like the old model of a counselor rather than a "mouthpiece" or an "attack dog" or a "hired gun." Hopefully, it will take root both substantively, in terms of changing lawyers' roles, and economically.

Returning to the problems at issue in this chapter, the solutions arc, unsurprisingly, a subject of debate in the legal community. Do the rules of procedure need to be fundamentally changed? Do judges just need to take hold of their cases and manage them more effectively? Or is it really the attorneys' fault: do they just need to cooperate in the pretrial phase of the case?

With respect to case management, some judges will say that they did not become judges to "manage" cases, but rather to try them; they will say that justice is not a widget and cannot be measured or calibrated; they will say that efficiency is not an appropriate goal. Then, too, some judges are simply indifferent to the effects of delay and are unwilling to jump in and aggressively manage a case. They have no interest in this approach. They view it as managerial mumbo jumbo, best suited to bureaucrats, not constitutional officers. Their reticence might be driven solely by numbers: they are carrying such a huge caseload that they could not possibly pay attention to each case. One judge from New York reported that if she actually managed each case, she would never go home. Another reason for resistance is the notion that since more than 90 percent of civil cases eventually settle, the judge should just leave all of the cases alone for a period of time and address the small percentage that demand attention. More granular reasons for the benign neglect of cases and caseflow management principles relate to lack of incentive (if one case is addressed efficiently, that just means that five more will arrive more quickly); concerns that some judges have about annoying or angering the lawyers and the consequent impact on election results; and the general overworked and underpaid syndrome.

With respect to rules changes, there are respected and accomplished attorneys and judges of the opinion that the mechanisms for addressing cost and delay are already contained within the existing Federal Rules and their state counterparts. In response to the various survey findings suggesting discontent with the pretrial discovery process, Magistrate Judge Paul Grimm of the US District Court for the District of Maryland is of the view that "it does not follow that a new round of comprehensive changes is the best or quickest way to achieve desired change."[31] Instead, any failure of the rules to rein in extensive and abusive discovery practices is "not expressive of a failure in the Rules themselves, but rather, must be viewed as an indictment of the parties, lawyers, and judges for allowing this to occur in the face of constraints that the Rules already provide."[32] Similarly, Judge Lee Rosenthal of the US District Court for the Southern District of Texas describes a "gap between the cup of the rules and the lip of judges, lawyers, and litigants applying them."[33] According to Judge Rosenthal, the solution lies not necessarily with rules changes, but rather in the idea that "reminding ourselves of the potential benefits available under the existing rules can provide the help that many are looking to obtain from new or different rules."[34]

Some commentators, most notably The Sedona Conference, a legal think tank geared toward practical solutions and recommendations, advocate for attorney cooperation as a means of reining in discovery practice and its associated time and costs. To this end, The Sedona Conference Cooperation Proclamation seeks to reduce the culture of adversarial discovery by providing judges and lawyers with resources in the form of toolkits that facilitate proportionality and cooperation in discovery practice. The hope is that lawyers will incorporate and judges endorse the recommendations in the Cooperation Proclamation. There are, of course, attorneys who eschew cooperation as a violation of their ethical obligation to represent their clients zealously, but a number of other observers or participants in the system note that good attorneys have always cooperated to some extent. It is the attorneys who resist that cooperation who need nudging.

All these threads weave into the tapestry of a solution, but in our view, rules reform is the weft of the fabric. The assumptions underlying the Federal Rules are anachronistic when applied to the increased speed, volume, and sophisticated technological demands of this brave new world we have to plumb in order to get to the truth. The rules were drafted for a time and litigation culture vastly different from those of today. In the words of Justice Broderick, "It's hard…to believe that if we were designing our court system from scratch today, to deal with the realities on the ground, that we would create the exact same model with the exact same paperwork."[35] It is time to roll up our collective sleeves and get to work on a new approach.

7

Changing the Process: It Is Time

In his 2010 state of the judiciary speech to the bench, bar, and citizens of Wyoming, Chief Justice Barton R. Voigt asked listeners: "Why would anyone prefer to get his justice from some tribunal held in the back room of a Holiday Inn rather than from the courts?"[1] His answer: "Because we are too slow and we are too expensive."[2] To reinvigorate the civil justice system and get the cases out of back rooms and into courtrooms, we must make changes. Now.

A construction defect case was filed in a small county in Colorado. The plaintiff—claiming she had been misled and that her home had structural defects—asked for damages and/or invalidation of the sale contract. Discovery and motions practice took almost two years. The case was scheduled for trial two years after it began, but trial was vacated when the case was transferred to bankruptcy court. The hearing was scheduled and rescheduled. At the time of this writing, it still has not occurred, after three years and many tens of thousands of dollars.

In North Carolina, husband and wife small-business owners got into a dispute with their landlord after the landlord locked them out of their business and turned off the electricity. The plaintiffs got a restraining order in court and brought suit for damages. Their breach of contract case took two and a half years, was spread over four or more judges and five hearings (and a loss of the record along the way which required that one hearing be repeated in full), and, although the business owners prevailed in their claim, they ended up owing money on account of the legal fees.

This is the face of modern litigation. To those who would counter by asserting that the United States has the best legal system in the world, we would interpose some caution. The World Justice Project released its 2010 *Rule of Law Index*, a study undertaken to assess the extent to which countries adhere to the rule of law. The report gauges country performance based on a number of factors that incorporate essential elements of the rule of law, including access to civil justice. Not surprisingly, the report found that countries in North America and Western Europe "tend to outperform most other countries in all dimensions," with the exception of accessibility of the civil justice system, particularly in the United States.[3] The US country report identified low scores in the following areas related to access to civil justice: (1) people can access and afford civil courts; (2) civil justice is impartial; and (3) civil justice is not subject to unreasonable delays.[4] Of the eleven countries grouped in the high-income category, the United States ranks last in access to civil justice.[5] The 2011 *Rule of Law Index* found the United States continued with high marks in most dimensions, but access continues to be an issue: "Legal assistance is expensive or unavailable...and the gap between rich and poor individuals in terms of both actual use of and satisfaction with the civil court system remains significant."[6]

For many years, the concerns about rapidly esca-
lating costs, legal gamesmanship, and long delays in
civil litigation provoked little more than grousing or
shoulder shrugs in the legal community. A sense of
cynicism, even fatalism, developed about the problems engulfing the courts. Lately, though, the tide has
begun to turn. For a number of reasons, there is now a
growing consensus among nearly all groups that participate in the system that the problems have reached
a tipping point. Change is inevitable. The time has
come for a feat many once thought impossible: a major
overhaul of our civil justice rules.

In May 2010, the federal Judicial Conference
committee responsible for considering and making
amendments to the Federal Rules held a national
conference at Duke University for the express purpose
of gathering insights and perspective from lawyers,
judges, and academics on how to improve the federal
litigation process in order to fulfill the goal of a "just,
speedy, and inexpensive determination of every action
and proceeding." The topics up for discussion included
discovery, e-discovery, pleadings, and motions, as well
as caseflow management, settlement, and lessons that
can be learned from a comparison between the federal
and state court systems. The conference drew more
than two hundred people: the movers and shakers of
the rules world—judges (state and federal), lawyers,
and academics. In short, most of the people who make
the decisions about what the rules should be.

Dozens of surveys and academic papers were prepared for and presented at the conference, designed to
help answer the remarkable question of what reforms
are necessary, practical, and appropriate to fix the civil
justice system. We have already spun the reader through

many of the survey results, and clearly the common thread is a deep dissatisfaction with the way things are working—not only among litigants, but increasingly among their attorneys and even the judges.

These concerns are not just cocktail party talk anymore, although there is still plenty of that. At the very least, there is a national consensus that the system really does cost too much and take too long. This is not justice. It is not the efficient search for the truth and resolution on the merits. It is not our grandparents' legal system envisioned by the drafters of the Federal Rules in the 1930s.

Something must change.

Another reason for the growing belief that change is not just possible but inevitable: other countries have done it. In England and Wales, significant reforms in the late 1990s resulted in an overhaul of the civil justice system, centered on a rewrite and unification of the rules of civil procedure. Lord Harry Woolf, former lord chief justice of England and Wales, the face behind these sweeping reforms, recognized that the key problems confronting the English civil justice system were cost, complexity, and delay resulting from unchecked adversarial practices. Lord Woolf considered the rules themselves to be the most appropriate avenue of reform, stating:

> It is often said that the existing rules and practice directions contain the solution to the present problems, if only litigation were to be conducted in accordance with them. But the present system does not ensure this. Instead the rules are flouted on a vast scale.[7]

The Woolf Reforms saw the advent of a procedure called "pre-action protocols" in England—an early mandatory process in which the parties exchange documents before ever filing the case. The reforms also institutionalized case management practices. These reforms were recently under review, and the Ministry of Justice is considering adjustments as appropriate.

In Canada, major reviews of the civil procedure rules have been undertaken in Ontario, British Columbia, and Alberta. On January 1, 2010, Ontario implemented a number of reforms, many of which are focused on concerns about proportionality (how the costs of litigation measure up against the amount in controversy or the importance of the lawsuit itself). Similar problems provided the impetus for rules reform in British Columbia, where reform interests also focused on proportionality, fairness, public confidence, and justice. The rules revisions took effect on July 1, 2010. The concerns prompting the review in Alberta were timeliness, affordability, and simplicity of civil court proceedings. The new rules of court were implemented on November 1, 2010.

This phenomenon of changes in court rules is not just occurring abroad. As early as the early 1990s, a very prescient chief justice, Thomas Zlaket of Arizona, saw the writing on the wall. He was an example of a judicial leader who changed a cultural climate (remember the dinosaurs). He commissioned a group of lawyers and judges to rethink the rules of civil procedure in order to respond to widespread concerns that the system was becoming unaffordable and increasingly "uncivilized, burdened with rudeness, untrustworthiness, hostility and bad manners."[8] The committee focused on discovery abuse, cost, delay, and a changing legal system that sharply diverged from that of the past. As Zlaket stated in 1993,

> a new generation of "litigators" who do not try cases has emerged. Indeed, a significant percentage of these attorneys would not even know how to try a case. What they know and do best is a great deal of discovery. Many do not recall, if they ever knew, that discovery was originally referred to as *pre-trial discovery*. It was one method, and certainly not the only one, by which trial lawyers prepared for the courtroom. Pre-trial discovery was not an end in itself, nor was it designed or intended to be a profit center for lawyers and law firms.[9]

That committee recommended sweeping changes to the Arizona Rules of Civil Procedure, including mandatory reciprocal disclosures and limits on experts, interrogatories, and depositions, which were ultimately adopted. IAALS has studied those changes and, eighteen years later, can now report on them. Only 25 percent of the bench and bar prefer Arizona federal court to state court.[10] Those who had litigation experience with the current rules and those in place prior to the changes in the early 1990s tend to prefer state court at a higher rate than those without such experience.[11] Furthermore, a plurality (49 percent) of those with experience under both sets of rules indicated that the amendments were a positive development for litigants, and a majority (55 percent) indicated the amendments were a positive development for lawyers.[12]

Oregon is another outlier. Oregon never bought into the dual premises of the Federal Rules—notice pleading and broad discovery. To the contrary, Oregon has rules that require specific fact-based pleading (rather than notice pleading) at the outset of the case and that do *not* allow for expert disclosure or reports. In short, Oregon courts require more detail at the outset about the facts sufficient to support a claim, and then they limit the discovery, including eliminating any discovery about expert witnesses. Lawyers from other states gasp at the very notion that a case could proceed in that fashion, but IAALS has studied that system as well and found that the Oregon bench and bar are champions of it. A plurality (43 percent) of respondents prefer Oregon state court to federal court, and when questioned about neighboring states, 68 percent preferred Oregon state court.[13]

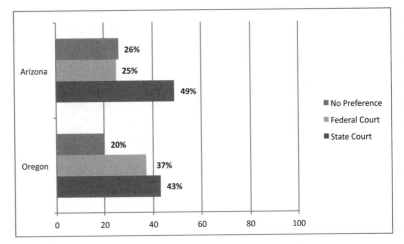

Statistics from 2010 IAALS surveys of the Arizona bench and bar and the Oregon bench and bar.

But that is all backdrop. Let's return to the last several years. Is there really a critical mass of will and information to support national change in the way cases are actually handled by the courts and by lawyers?

The American College of Trial Lawyers and IAALS have been at the forefront of this movement.

Armed and informed by survey data and research from around the world, the ACTL Task Force on Discovery and Civil Justice began thinking about solutions. That conversation led to a proposed set of recommendations (American College/IAALS Principles) that would guide rules reform. There are twenty-nine of them, but broadly, they bunch into the following areas:

1. *Proportionality.* One size does not fit all. Every case should not be entitled to or required to undergo the same procedures as every other case. Making a bicycle takes different tools than making a motorcycle. This principle can be seen in the differentiated case management approach or in the employment case protocols, discussed below.

2. *Fact-based pleading.* The parties need to put their best feet forward early in the litigation. Plaintiffs need to plead facts supporting their claims, and defendants need to plead facts supporting their defenses. The days of merely requiring the party to state enough to put the other side on notice of the claim should be over. This principle is intended to narrow the focus of the lawsuit at an early point in time so that the rest of the pretrial process is more efficient and cost-effective.

3. *Disclosures.* To get the ball rolling, each party should hand over the documents and a list of witnesses that support their claims or defenses shortly after the lawsuit begins. After that, only limited discovery should be allowed—discovery proportionately tied to the claims actually at issue.

4. *Discovery.* Discovery should be a means to an end—not an end unto itself. It should promote the just, speedy, and inexpensive resolution of a case.

Not all facts should be discoverable; not all tools of discovery should be deployed in every case.

This is a radical departure from current discovery practices. As attorney Gordon Netzorg of the American College Task Force says: "We need to change the discovery paradigm from the 'all-you-can-eat' model to you get what you need."[14]

The recommended limits on discovery can run the gamut from limits on interrogatories or depositions (numbers and length) to a complete ban on expert depositions or requests for admission.

5. *Caseflow management.* Judges need to intervene early in the pretrial process and actively manage the case. One judge should handle a case from start to finish, set a firm trial date at an early point in time, and prioritize resolution of motions.

Some of these principles require rules changes, while others require only an application of caseflow management best practices.

As to that latter piece of the puzzle, IAALS's recommended path for judges to lead the system toward greater effectiveness reads like a manifesto of common sense, but it is actually the synthesized result of well-trod research and the experiences of trial judges and lawyers from around the country:

1. *Schedules matter.* Firm dates should be set early in the pretrial process for the close of discovery, the filing of dispositive motions, and trial—and those dates should be maintained, except in truly unusual circumstances.

2. *Rulings rule.* Motions should be ruled on quickly, sometimes even without the need for actual filings,

but rather just telephonic hearings.

Relating his experience as an attorney, American College Task Force member and Ohio federal court judge Jack Zouhary laments: "Oftentimes as a trial lawyer, you got to the point where, please, even if you rule against me, just rule! Make a decision, because being in limbo was worse."[15]

3. *Extensions must be rare.* Extensions of deadlines or trial dates must be limited in number and duration. A culture of extensions means slower, more expensive case resolution.

4. *Preaching must reach the choir and beyond.* A local legal culture that accepts efficient case processing as the norm must be fostered and judicial leadership is key to achieving that culture.

5. *What gets measured gets managed.* The status of cases and motions must be tracked through internal statistical reporting, and it is to the system's and society's mutual benefit that the vast majority of such results be publicly available.

Two caveats should be noted as we breeze through the caseflow management jungle like visitors on a Disney World ride. First, a sea change cannot be affected by fiat: judges are of essentially equal status in most courts. A judge in a leadership position, such as a presiding judge, is often described as "first among equals" and has limited formal authority to set administrative policy for the court. As a consequence, particular case management practices—even those deemed to be best practices—cannot simply be mandated.

However, the role of a strong judicial leader is critical. Judges learn from each other, compete with each other, and listen to each other. Caseflow management does not happen without judicial leadership, but sometimes that leadership is quite decentralized.

Second, precisely because the bench is marked by autonomy, case management cannot be an informal process or project—it must be institutionalized to be sustainable. One judge can put cutting-edge case management practices in place, but when that judge leaves and another arrives, it is all for naught. This is true because turnover and attrition can make the system one of men, not laws. Case management is one part of the antidote to delayed justice and mounting costs, but it is not enough by itself. Judges must be managing within a clear framework, and that framework must include revised rules of civil procedure.

The buck stops elsewhere as well. Attorneys, too, play a role in resolving cases more quickly for their clients. Again, the suggestions look simplistic but are actually supported by the data:

1. *Defer to deadlines.* Early in the case, realistic deadlines should be agreed to, and seeking deviations should be sought only under unusual circumstances.
2. *Dispatch discovery.* Discovery must be commenced early in the discovery period, so that any discovery disputes may be presented to the court and resolved well before the discovery deadline. E-discovery issues in particular must be addressed at the earliest possible point in the litigation—before costs begin to escalate unnecessarily.
3. *File with urgency.* Motions that could dispose of the case or part of the case without a trial (motions to dismiss or for summary judgment) should be made as early as possible in the case.

4. *Collaborate without fear.* Attorneys need to approach
   the pretrial process as one that demands collaboration, not charge into the ring from opposing cor-
   ners. Consider plaintiffs in the Superior Court of
   Arizona who filed a motion with the court seeking to compel opposing counsel to have lunch. The
   court, noting that it had "rarely seen a motion with
   more merit," granted the plaintiffs' motion.[16]

We have explored the specific role of judges and
attorneys in creating efficient case processing, and,
in sum, what the research shows is that certain small
changes easily within the ability of an individual judge
or attorney—such as simply changing the first date on
which the court pays attention to the case or resolving
pending motions more quickly—can have a significant and expanding impact over the life of a case. For
example, if a judge resolves pending motions quickly,
other deadlines stay in place and the case moves
ahead. If, on the other hand, motions languish, the
ripple effect bumps almost every other deadline, and
there are motions to extend the deadlines, opposition
to those motions, and so on.

Other changes, though more complex and requiring broader cultural and systemic reform, have been
readily identified as well. The clear conclusion: efficient case processing is most likely to occur where the
local legal community—steered by the expectations
and leadership of the judiciary—embraces (or at least
accepts) strong case management. Efficient courts
move quickly at *every* stage of the case. The fastest
courts in overall time to disposition are also the fastest courts in processing at each stage of the litigation,
and the slowest courts overall are the slowest courts

at each stage of litigation. So reducing delay in the courtroom, then, does not appear to be a matter of addressing one or two specific pretrial practices, but rather striving to shorten the time between events at every stage of the case. Judges must take hold of their cases, triage them in order to provide the attention that each case requires, then set and enforce firm expectations. Conversely, attorneys must be clear as to what the court expects of them, and they must follow through with their obligations in a timely and efficient manner. This approach comports with the research and American College/IAALS Principles suggesting that one size does not fit all when it comes to cases and that proportionality must be the goal.

The balance of the recommendations in the Principles would require actual changes to the rules of procedure. Those changes cannot happen on a case-by-case basis or at the direction of one judge or one chief judge. They require far more systemic and cultural change. It is a tall order. But from our point of view, the best news is that these Principles and all of the papers, reports, and findings are not gathering dust on a shelf. Things are actually happening, changes are being made.

The locus for the changes is primarily the state courts because of their agility and flexibility; the federal courts are constrained by a mandate of uniformity, which, to a certain extent, reduces their capacity to experiment. The state courts have no such constraints. During 2010, pilot projects to test new ways of structuring a civil justice system, including various parts of the American College/IAALS Principles, have been put in place, and other courts are currently in the process of developing their own pilot projects.

These projects share many of the same goals and objectives: to address the increasing burden of discovery, particularly in the electronic age, and to ensure a system that is efficient, affordable, and accessible. The applicable rules range from the modest to the expansive—some requiring mandatory exchange of information between the parties at the outset followed by limited discovery, and others controlling the use of experts and the associated depositions. At this point, pilot projects seem to be gaining steam as lawyers and judges struggle to fix the system.

Although pilot projects and rules changes have been taking place in states for decades now, because of the increased role of empirical data in making decisions about proposed rule amendments, these projects are likely to be different. Collecting data about rules changes and their impact is a very important step. Although change is imperative, venturing into major changes without some experimentation might be irresponsible. According to the University of Richmond School of Law's Carl Tobias, "No individual or institution…can know exactly how the new provisions will in fact operate until judges have employed them, lawyers and litigants have attempted to comply with the measures, and the devices have received careful scrutiny."[17]

The National Center for State Courts and IAALS are committed to measuring some of the state pilot projects and have developed a measurement protocol for that purpose. The intent is that by 2013 there will be a sufficient database collected from the pilot project jurisdictions to guide future changes with the benefit of twenty-twenty hindsight.

Rules set the standard and draw the map for civil litigation. Civil litigation is dysfunctional; thus, the map must be changed. What we do not know yet is what the right map looks like, and, indeed, there might be no one right answer. Even if it seems swift and sure, none of us wants to ride off on a horse without a sense of where it will eventually take us. The answer is to experiment with solutions that broad groups of stakeholders have designed, and then share data across various jurisdictions so that success can be institutionalized and we can begin to regain a system that provides a "just, speedy, and inexpensive" process.

8
Divorce Court

It seems that the wag who once said "marriage is grand—divorce is a hundred grand" was underestimating the situation.

Consider the Wolf couple's divorce in Cuyahoga County, Ohio, which was filed in July 2004. When the *Cleveland Plain Dealer* published a list of protracted divorce cases in August 2008, the Wolf case was still open and some $350,000 in attorney fees had been billed during the intervening four years.[1] The Granger divorce began in September 2000, with $240,000 of fees amassed, but eight years later, the matter was still unresolved.[2] The Halliday couple filed their divorce in March 2003, and by August 2008 the combined attorney fees had reached $350,000.[3] In Colorado, a recent divorce case involving a five-year marriage and no children dragged on for four years and cost in excess of $1 million in attorney fees and costs. The ultimate award of marital assets was $100,000, so the cost of the proceeding was about $700 per day, and $10,000 was spent for every $1 awarded. How about that for cost-effectiveness?[4]

Furthermore, the problems with domestic relations cases do not end when the final decree of divorce enters. Far from it. Some cases linger for years, and the parties use judges or other court personnel as their tools of torture to continue to whittle away at the other party's resources and well-being. In one case, the process leading up to the decree was contentious and expensive. The two parties were at each other's throats, with a young girl, their only child, in the middle. The trial judge assumed that the controversy would abate once the decree entered, if for no other reason than the costs of litigation. It did not. The father began to represent himself, but things continued in the form of motion after motion from both sides. He did not pay child support; she did not provide parenting time as ordered. He made derogatory statements about her, in violation of the terms of the decree; she permitted the child to do things that he disapproved of. The parents were of two different religions, and the most fertile ground for conflict between them related to whether the child would go to one place of worship or the other, whether she would be called by her first name or her middle name (each one from different religious traditions), whether her hair would be cut or left long. It went on and on. The trial judge developed a system of resolving their disputes that involved immediate telephonic hearings where she would hear the two sides, make a decision, and enter a Minute Order in the record in an effort to minimize the delays and costs. But, at some point, the trial judge was enabling their unwillingness to face up to the situation and figure out how to resolve it themselves. The process itself became part of their coping mechanism.

Consider another case in which the parties resolved the initial divorce with an agreed-upon separation agreement and entry of decree after nine months, but between 1998 and 2009, there were approximately thirty post-decree motions concerning parenting time and child-related expenses. The father retains his same attorney, but the mother has had seven attorneys, and there were five experts to assess and evaluate parenting time issues. Three judges and one magistrate have heard matters in this case. The children, now eighteen and twenty-one, have known nothing but conflict between their parents since ages four and seven. Clearly these examples are not a good way to run a system—for anyone.

These might seem like extraordinary cases, but litigation costs and delay in divorce and custody cases regularly deplete family resources and leave the parties and their children in financial ruin. Some families never recover from this experience with the litigation process—financially or emotionally.

Almost everyone understands the problem's ubiquity from personal experience or close affiliation. According to the National Center for Health Statistics, the November 2009 rate of divorce in the United States was 3.4 per 1,000 people.[5] Although the divorce rate has decreased since 1970,[6] it is still one of the highest rates in the industrialized world.[7] "Slightly more than half of all divorces involve children under the age of eighteen," and approximately "40 percent of all children will experience parental divorce before reaching" the age of majority.[8]

Cohabitation has complicated the picture. The most recent National Center for Health Statistics numbers show that almost 49 percent of men and 50 percent of women between the ages of fifteen and forty-four have cohabited (defined as living with someone of the opposite sex, in a sexual relationship, outside of marriage).[9] More significant in terms of social and legal impacts is the fact that as of 2002, 55 percent of cohabiting men and 59 percent of cohabiting women had a biological child.[10] A recent study by the Pew Research Center found an eightfold increase over the last fifty years in the percentage of children born to unmarried mothers—from 5 percent in 1960 to the current figure of 41 percent.[11]

Cohabiting partners might never need to seek court involvement—unless they have children. On the other hand, cohabiting partners, even if never formally married, might need to seek court resolution for issues of custody, visitation, and child support. Minnesota state court judge Bruce Peterson says that in his district, cases involving unmarried parents outnumber those of married parents. "And I assume," he says, "that is also true around the country."[12]

Further complicating the process is the evolution of law and practice regarding custody and parenting time decision making. Historically, there was a paternal preference that then gave way to a presumption that children needed their mothers more than their fathers during the so-called tender years. More recently this evolution has reflected a cultural shift of much greater involvement of fathers in their children's lives, resulting in legal presumptions of joint custody and fifty-fifty shared parenting time. The most common legal standard that judges must apply in determining where children will reside, which parent will make decisions about their lives, and how the children will spend time with both parents going forward is the "best interests of the child" standard. Faced with the impossible task of predicting behavior and assessing a child's needs, courts and parents have turned to a stable of various mental health and attorney experts to advise the decision. The addition of these often dueling experts has only increased the cost and delay in divorces, not only in the initial process, but often in the years of post-decree motions.

In the past decade, state courts have experienced a steady growth in domestic relations case filings, which include cases comprising all of the financial and cus-todial disputes between spouses and married or never-married parents. According to the National Center for State Courts, domestic relations caseloads between 1999 and 2008 increased by 8 percent.[13] Some of the most dramatic increases relate to custody and support matters. The NCSC also reports that between 1999 and 2008, custody filings increased by 20 percent, and support filings increased by 26 percent in those states surveyed as part of the Court Statistics Project.[14] In Georgia Superior Courts, for example, domestic rela-tions cases outnumber all the other civil cases filed, as well as all felony and misdemeanor criminal cases.[15] It is not surprising, therefore, that Georgia courts devote more time to domestic relations cases than to criminal cases (both felony and misdemeanor cases combined).[16] Retired Georgia Supreme Court jus-tice Leah Ward Sears cautions, "While the problem may not lend itself to headlines and 30-second sound bites on the evening news, that does not mean we do not have a family law caseload problem in our courts, because we do."[17]

Bear in mind that those least capable of dealing with the status quo's failings are its greatest victims: the children of separating parents. Popular and aca-demic literature is replete with stories and studies identifying negative impacts of divorce and sepa-ration on children. These range from increased risk for school dropout to teen pregnancy and substance abuse. More to the point, evidence is ample that children who experience a high-conflict divorce—with protracted and expensive court involvement—tend to suffer even more, in both the short and long term.

"The adversarial system is as bad a system as you could design for family litigation," says Judge Peterson.

> It entrenches opposition, takes away responsibility for resolving the conflict, and creates the illusion of winners and losers. The adversarial system works for determining what has occurred in the past, when someone is trying to prove something that happened to someone, but most family court decisions are about the future, planning for things that will change, especially regarding children. And the adversarial system is just very poorly suited to handle that.[18]

Divorce and custody disputes deeply disrupt not only American families, but also commerce and the culture at large. Less compelling emotionally, but compelling nonetheless, is the impact of the failed divorce system on American business. It is intuitive that home life and work life are emotionally intertwined; pretending that they are separable is both unnatural and unhealthy. Any observant business leader can tell you that an employee's problems at home can increase absenteeism, decrease productivity, and worsen safety in the workplace.

The most substantive analysis to date, a 1996 study entitled *Associations Between Marital Distress and Work Loss in a National Sample*,[19] found that "higher levels of marital conflict on one day strongly predicted lower levels of work productivity the next day."[20] The authors of this study extrapolated a loss of 1.34 days per month of work due to marital distress, compared to workers who had average levels of marital conflict.[21] This translated to more than $1,400 in lost earnings per year, for a total of $6.8 billion per year for the entire United States.[22]

David G. Schramm's study of 9,735 divorces in Utah in 2001, built on the 1996 work loss study, looked to determine direct and indirect costs incurred by individuals going through a divorce, as well as resultant costs incurred by state and federal government. The author's subsequent estimation brought the total direct and indirect costs of divorce for the United States to $33.3 billion annually.[23]

Now, all of these data could support a simple conclusion: either that people should not get married, or that they should not get divorced. Neither conclusion is likely to gain any traction. People will marry and have children, and some will separate. How society chooses to orchestrate the separation process is the question at hand, and our premise is that it is orchestrated with very little attention to the musicians.

The adversarial process is ideal for the criminal justice system, where out of the crucible of cross-examination comes truth. It also is workable for civil cases, particularly those in which the parties will have no ongoing involvement with each other. In divorce cases, however, adversary litigation strikes a sour note. Whereas the general civil justice system needs merely to be reconstructed on its existing foundation, the American way of divorce and proceedings dealing with never-married parent custody and financial disputes need to be razed and redesigned. Consider

the extent to which family-related matters comprise
some states' dockets: in 2006, family and juvenile cases
accounted for nearly 46 percent of the total filings in
Maryland; family law cases were 58 percent of the trial
court caseload in Nebraska; and family-related cases
were 49 percent of the state trial docket in Nevada.[24]

In divorce cases, the goal should be to separate two
parties' lives with as little negative impact as possible
on their children, finances, and ability to communicate with one another. The current structure abjectly
fails to meet that goal. Keep in mind that our society allows business partners to divide up their businesses and go their separate ways without the need
for the approval of the court. Those business disputes
only go to court if they cannot reach agreement. The
system requires divorcing parties to go to court even
when they do agree, and it requires judges to exercise
an almost parental oversight function in measuring
whether the division of assets and parental responsibilities is appropriate. Given the damage the process
causes, the costs of mandating court involvement out-
weigh the benefits.

The traditional court process also has other unintended consequences that extend beyond the parties and their families and impact the court system
itself. Most judges have no interest or experience in a
domestic relations docket and might display an atti-
tude of simply serving their time on those cases. The
all-too-common term for a domestic relations docket
among judges is *pots and pans*, because judges see it
as merely a process of dividing up the pots and pans
between warring parties. Frequently, multiple judges
will handle one case, resulting in increased expense,
delay, and inconsistency.

Many of the parties in domestic relations proceedings do not have attorneys. In fact, the number of self-represented litigants in these case types is breathtakingly high. In 2003, the rate of self-represented individuals in California family law cases averaged 67 to 72 percent.[25] In Utah, 49 percent of petitioners and 81 percent of respondents in divorce cases were self-represented in 2005.[26] And the numbers have since been rising. As a result, the courts must serve and adapt to litigants who are completely unfamiliar with court processes. A major reason for this is fiscal. Parties who wish to have counsel but are indigent can seldom find attorneys or legal service groups that will take their cases. Other parties who might have the money to hire an attorney choose not to do so, worrying that the attorneys will both complicate the case and drain their resources at a critical time in their lives (and the lives of their children).

As for consistency of administration across the states, forget it. Different laws, rules, and procedures abound. There are different waiting periods, different expert designations, different available resources in every state. These cases are heard in some jurisdictions by a single judge; other jurisdictions have designed dedicated family courts to rule on all matters impacting families in a holistic manner; and in yet others they are handled in an uncoordinated way by multiple state courts and judges having jurisdiction over sundry, separate matters affecting one family. Particularly for a self-represented litigant, sorting out what the process requires might be overwhelming and tedious.

And so we find ourselves in a vicious cycle. Case filings are rising, the number of self-represented litigants is increasing, the demographics of those seeking assistance from the courts are changing dramatically, and court resources are shrinking. The bottom line is that the judges are unhappy, the litigants are very unhappy, and the ramifications for the court system itself are severe. Recognizing the breadth and severity of the problem, it is now time to evaluate new approaches and implement reforms in the court process itself and also establish out-of-court resources to provide alternative, nonadversarial avenues for the resolution of family matters.

There have been various movements in the handling of family court cases over the last two decades. They range from the establishment of unified family courts dealing with family issues holistically to an emphasis on court-ordered mediation for dispute resolution in the family context, from case management models to a rich service-provider model designed to give the families access to a variety of services as they make their way through the courts.

Among the most thoughtful advocates of family court reform is Barbara A. Babb, associate professor of law at the University of Baltimore School of Law and director of its Center for Families, Children and the Courts. Babb promotes a vision of "therapeutic jurisprudence" that seeks to get rid of old adversarial fault-based models. "It's not about deciding winners and losers," says Babb, rather

> it's a problem-solving approach where the goal is to improve the lives of the various family members. A second theoretical construct here is looking holistically at the family unit—not simply husband or wife or child, but seeking a complete picture that would answer a fuller question like "how can you

increase the parents' involvement in the child's schooling to strengthen their relationship?"[27]

Surprisingly, Babb is dubious about some reformers' promotion of a "one judge, one family" approach, because she worries about any single overseer wittingly or unwittingly acquiring a bias for or against various family members. But she is adamant about the need for "one judge, one case," where the same judge hears a case from start to finish, or "one family, one team," where the same family court administrative team sees the family each time they come to court. Babb sees five features as crucial to unified family courts, the court structure she promotes:

First, that it is a court of general jurisdiction with the same level of powers as a civil and criminal court. Second, that there is early and active case management, with links to family services. Third, that the service system, while court-supplied or court-connected and with definite reporting requirements, realizes that the *non*-legal issues— and here I'm thinking mental health, substance abuse, poverty, homelessness—are often more important in family law cases than the underlying dispute. Fourth, that the court have comprehensive jurisdiction, being able to hear a full range of family law cases from custody to child support and property but also abuse and neglect and delinquency. That's the one system, one family idea. Last, the system has to be user-friendly—especially with so many unrepresented litigants—it has to be accessible and navigable, and that's a real challenge.[28]

Trying to improve the existing system, various jurisdictions within the United States and abroad have addressed domestic relations in a number of ways, some paralleling Babb's thinking:

- Simplifying the domestic relations court procedures
- Court-sponsored mediation
- Court-sponsored early neutral evaluation programs for both parenting and financial issues
- Court-sponsored counseling services
- Designating or selecting judges for this specific docket
- Judicial education for these designated judges, both before and after assuming the domestic relations docket
- Judicial rotation policies that promote consistency and development of expertise in this area of law
- Use of case managers/family court facilitators to provide guidance and assistance to litigants at the front end of the court process and consistently thereafter—sort of coaches for the parties.

Some jurisdictions use a variety of these techniques, while others use just one or two; some focus on children, some focus on the entire family unit, while still others attempt to change the legal culture itself. A handful of noteworthy approaches have emerged in recent years.

Many jurisdictions have specialized rules and procedures for domestic relations cases. For example, Colorado's rule creates a process whereby the parties have access to a judge or family court facilitator early in the process and on a consistent basis throughout the case, so as to address issues promptly and with a minimum of paperwork and posturing.[29] Critical to the process is a new court staff position, called a family court facilitator, designed to assist the parties, even on an individual basis, with moving the case through the system. The vision of Rule 16.2 is to keep the primary responsibility for making decisions within the family itself, to use the court system only as absolutely necessary on an issue-by-issue basis, but in a very efficient and targeted way.

Florida is one of a number of states that has instituted a Unified Family Court system that is meant to be a fully integrated, comprehensive approach to resolving family disputes in a fair, efficient, cost-effective manner. The essential components include active case management by the court, coordination of any cases involving the same family, collaboration between the court and community to provide access to services for families, and a less adversarial approach to family cases.[30]

In Connecticut, the family services program uses a family civil intake screen to assess the level of family conflict and complexity of the issues and then provides for appropriate differentiated case management and interventions for each family—including dispute resolution services, evaluations, and education.[31]

DC's Family Court Act provides that an individual may not serve on the family court or handle a family court case unless he or she has training or expertise in family law and certifies that they intend to serve the full five-year term of service.[32] In addition, the court actively identifies and recruits associate judges interested in serving on the family court and who have the requisite education and professional background required by the act.

Mediation is required in California and must be set before or concurrently with the setting of the matter for hearing by the court. The purposes of the mediation proceeding are "(1) to reduce acrimony that might exist between the parties, (2) to develop an agreement assuring that the child has close and continuing contact with both parents when in the best interest of the child, and...(3) to effect a settlement of the issue of visitation rights of all parties that is in the best interest of the child."[33] Many court systems provide court-annexed mediation services on a sliding fee basis to individuals who have filed cases with the court.

The United States is not alone in tailoring unique rules and procedures to domestic relations cases. Singapore's Family Relations Chambers (FRC) is a one-stop center within the family court, providing opportunities for families and couples to resolve their disputes in a nontrial setting.[34] The FRC is an integral unit of the family court, with a dedicated multidisciplinary team of judges, counselors, and support staff. The FRC offers various services: family violence assessment and counseling; individual support counseling; divorce counseling; divorce mediation; custody and access evaluation; and maintenance mediation.

While commendable and innovative, these programs are only available to a couple that has filed for divorce (or other court order) and not to a couple that is still in the throes of trying to weigh their options. In the United States, prefiling resources are currently available to families only on a scattershot basis around the country. Some out-of-court programs are available in US jurisdictions, such as Connecticut, but there, as elsewhere, access is typically provided only *after* a case has been filed with the court. Coordinated, comprehensive out-of-court resources available to families before they ever cross the courthouse threshold are rare. The goal of such programs is the resolution of family disputes outside of and prior to engaging the adversarial court system (even if papers must ultimately be filed with the court to finalize the process).

Australia and British Columbia are among the few jurisdictions that have experimented with establishing completely out-of-court models to assist families experiencing difficulties or contemplating divorce. These models provide education, communication skills, and dispute resolution alternatives to help the families come to agreement on their issues. The focus of these models revolves around issues that impact children and a resultant effort to minimize negative impact.

The system in Australia, Family Relationship Centres, provides a first port of call for families and is available before the filing of any court action. The centers are designed to help families strengthen relationships and deal with relationship difficulties. They provide families with information, advice, and dispute resolution services to help them reach an agreement on parenting arrangements without going to court. The range of services and programs supports families at all stages, including people starting relationships, those wanting to make their relationships stronger, those having relationship difficulties, and those affected when families separate. The program includes a systematic monitoring and evaluation process of the centers themselves. One goal is to reduce the number of filings in court by providing resources for people to address and resolve their relationship issues. For cases that *are* filed, the goal is to provide avenues for families to reach agreement on all or most issues—or, at the very least, remain outside of the adversarial process—before they file. An evaluation of the program was undertaken in 2009, finding overall that "there is more use of relationship services, a decline in filings in the courts in children cases, and a shift away from an automotive recourse to solutions sought through legal processes in response to post-separation relationship difficulties."[35]

British Columbia's Family Justice Centres (FJCs) are designed to provide a variety of services that permit parties going through marital or relationship conflict to avoid having to go to court. These services include family justice counselor dispute resolution; parenting after separation counseling; comprehensive child support services; assessments and referrals; and enforcement outreach.[36] The goal of these services is to reduce the demands on the family court system. These services are provided free of charge, and client participation with an FJC is generally voluntary, although a few provincial courts mandate meetings with a family justice counselor before a first hearing with a judge. Courts may also order custody and access assessments from counselors, and parties can meet with counselors for assistance in reaching agreements instead of first going to court.

In the United States, there are private lawyers, therapists, and mediators who specialize in providing services to couples contemplating divorce. Just as with court-sponsored mediation services, these private providers attempt to reduce the need for court hearings by working through contentious issues outside of the court system. This is definitely not one-stop shopping: each of the involved professionals has a specific purpose and specialty and will attempt either to help the parties work through their problems or reach agreement in anticipation of divorce.

Included in this mix of solutions to the problem of the divorce process is collaborative law. This is a relatively new process, designed to resolve family disputes without the stress, delay, and expense of litigation. The process involves face-to-face meetings, with each spouse represented by a specially trained lawyer. The meetings are dedicated to identifying and addressing the issues needing to be resolved. In the event that either spouse wishes to litigate the dispute in court, both spouses are required to hire new lawyers. This is a critical feature of the process that motivates everyone involved to continue working toward a mutually agreeable resolution. Mediators, financial planners, divorce coaches, child specialists, and other conflict resolution professionals may be involved in the collaborative divorce process. The professionals work together to get the parties divorced without the hostility, emotional harm, and depletion of resources that can accompany a long, drawn-out court battle. Although the movement has gained momentum, as with private mediation services, the cost of hiring collaborative law attorneys—and additional attorneys if the process fails—can be prohibitive for those with limited budgets.

In the mid-1990s, some 80 percent of Fortune 500 companies were reported to provide some form of employee assistance programs,[37] and a 2004 article in *Employee Assistance Quarterly* reports that more than 90 percent of all Fortune 500 companies offered employee assistance programs as part of basic benefits packages. Of employers surveyed in the Families and Work Institute's *2008 National Study of Employers*,

65 percent provide employee assistance programs.[38] These programs generally offer on-site assistance to employees to address personal issues including marital, family, and relationship issues that might affect job performance. These programs deal with the effects of dissolution or other family issues, but do nothing to help the individuals understand the court process or negotiate it if necessary.

The bottom line is that the divorce process uses "Jaws of Life" to separate couples, when a simple open door might suffice, and the collateral damage from that miscalculation is just unacceptable. Too much is at stake to allow the status quo to remain static. With so many promising models available around the world, and even around the country, the challenge now is for jurisdictions to customize and import best practices, with continuous evaluation and sharing of information about how the programs are working on the ground so that they can be adjusted as needed. Again, this effort should embrace both a court-processing model and an out-of-court model.

The purpose of changes to the in-court process should be to minimize the adversarial approach to litigation and create a system that is speedy, simple, inexpensive, and fair. Some of the principles IAALS supports are:

- Early intervention in the case by a judge
- Limited discovery
- Limited court appearances: in number and duration
- A court's physical facilities being easy to navigate and accommodating working people with families (although it sounds like heresy—how about evening and weekend court hours?)

- Adequate staff support for the judge
- All domestic relations cases being resolved within twelve months of filing
- Training, training, training—for the judges and court staff
- Measuring reforms and sharing that data

As for taking cases outside of the court system altogether, it is time for the United States to initiate a series of pilot projects based on the family relationship centers in Australia and British Columbia. Such initiatives can offer a one-stop resource where attorneys, tax specialists, financial planners, mediators, and mental health experts specializing in children and family issues are housed in the same location. Trained staff could conduct an initial assessment to educate and direct parties to appropriate services available in the center. Sliding scale fees could be made available, so that the systems could serve all income levels. Imagine the difference it would make if there were one place where parties contemplating divorce could get all the information and assistance they might need to figure out how to divide up their lives, their finances, and their parenting responsibilities. Imagine further that this location would encourage the parties to take the reins and figure out what might be best for their family, rather than polarizing, fighting, recording one another's phone calls, and demanding discovery of e-mails. Even if papers ultimately still have to be filed in a court to dissolve the marriage or to enter enforceable financial orders, working out the issues in advance of that filing will be to everyone's advantage.

And if the process did not involve the courts at all, if a divorce decree could be filed with the clerk and recorder like a business dissolution and only in court if one party was not living up to the agreement, would that be so bad? The courts would not miss these cases, and our guess is that the families would not miss the courts. In fact, our guess is that the great bulk of the cases would be handled far more appropriately, and only the small percentage of high-conflict divorce cases or divorces posing irresolvable issues would still make their way into court.

For his part, Minnesota's Judge Peterson contends that the challenge is of great significance to society. The population of individuals needing these services is growing and changing, and the courts need to change to provide for them. Judge Peterson cautions:

> We're talking about a growing population of unmarried parents. Many of these did not plan to be parents together, some even deny that they *are* parents, and many face barriers, such as poverty, instability, and high-conflict relationships, to being effective parents. We can't afford to continue with a system that just isn't equipped to help them. And much the same could be said of the more traditional divorce cases where conflict can be reduced through better management. This is in everyone's interest.[39]

As for Babb—whose center is currently partnering with the Family Law Section of the American Bar Association to push a Families Matter Initiative to advance many of the ideas expressed above—she shares Peterson's sense of urgency. "Look, families are always going to go through separations," she says, "but you can use collaboration and attention to families' and children's needs to better protect everybody concerned and minimize the suffering. Tragic examples need to become the exception, not the rule. That's only going to happen with family justice system reform. And that reform is only going to happen with judicial leadership at the top level."[40]

9

Insiders Speak

On the subject of judicial leadership, we want to give voice here to some of those leaders.[1] There are approximately 1,500 federal judges in this country and around 27,000 state court judges. These judges are, as we have noted, the heart and soul of the court system. Many (if not most) of them are truly extraordinary people, dedicated public servants who care deeply about our system of justice. They are the ones who animate and operate the system, and we want you to hear some of their ideas and frustrations—from them. We also want you to hear from some of the individuals who actually run the systems: the court administrators. It is the partnership between the really capable administrators and the really capable judges that forges effective leadership and causes real change to occur.

We begin with three federal district court judges, the trial court judges of the federal system: David Campbell, a district court judge in Arizona; Jack Zouhary in Ohio; and Mark Bennett in Iowa. All three have common concerns and common approaches to the solutions.

Cost and Delay

First, they think the civil litigation system is bloated. Judge Campbell, who came to the bench from a complex civil litigation practice, notes some stark comparisons between a criminal case and a civil case:

> I've concluded that a lot of what we think in our
> civil litigation system is good lawyering is a waste
> of time. And I've learned that, I think most dra-
> matically, from looking at the contrast between
> criminal cases and civil cases: well, more specifi-
> cally criminal trials and civil trials. You know, I'll
> sit through a two-week criminal trial—there will
> be one prosecutor and one defense lawyer, maybe
> with a paralegal. The criminal defense lawyer will
> mark fifty exhibits and use forty-seven of them;
> the criminal defense lawyer will very effectively
> cross-examine witnesses he has never deposed. I
> can sit through a two-week civil trial and there
> will be three lawyers on each side of the court-
> room. The defense will mark 350 exhibits and use
> 47 of them. The defense lawyers will have stacks
> of heavily annotated depositions for every witness
> that comes into the courtroom, which virtually
> never make a difference in the case. In fact, I com-
> pared two cases last year: The criminal defense
> lawyer where liberty is on the line will incur fees
> of $50,000 or $75,000, and the civil litigators
> in a significant bet-the-company case will incur
> ten times that much. And so, I have come to the
> view that we really—if the goal is fair dispute
> resolution, we really overlitigate civil cases sys-
> temically…You know, we are willing to put liberty
> on the line with lawyers who have never taken a
> deposition, and yet, there are very few civil litiga-
> tors who would ever think of walking into a court-
> room to question a witness they hadn't deposed.

Judge Campbell thinks the lawyers should be asking themselves: what do I need to win in front of a jury, and how do I most efficiently go get it and put it together for a jury trial? Instead, they are currently asking: what discovery do I need to do?

He attributes the problem in large part to stakeholder culture—the lawyers, the judges, and the clients—and he points to the Eastern District of Virginia, where the culture is different. There, cases move quickly, and the participants have acclimated to those expectations. Judge Campbell says, "I am sure there are some costs that get front-loaded in cases in the Eastern District, but I'll bet that on average if they're resolving [cases] in about half the time, they are doing it for half the cost."

Judge Campbell, for his part, puts civil cases on faster schedules and actively manages them at every step. He imposes substantive, significant limits on discovery. He does not grant extensions unless really warranted, and he resolves issues promptly.

Judge Zouhary sees the same problem and has a similar approach to the solution. What leaves a bad taste in Judge Zouhary's mouth? "Costs of our legal system right now and timeliness. Cases take too long and cost too much. And as a result, a lot of people are being shut out of the system." He, like Judge Campbell, is committed to case management. He has put together his top-ten list of case management techniques, and he constantly revisits his own practices with a view toward improvement.

Judge Bennett is another proponent of active case management, observing that there should be early, very firm trial dates in each case, a reduced amount of discovery, and a shortened time from filing to trial.

He also encourages either eliminating summary judgment or changing the standard to make it, in reality, "more difficult to obtain" and "shifting the costs when it is denied." He identifies the need for "staff that takes public service as seriously as the judges; a well-defined mission statement for the court; judges with an unfailing willingness to help each other; and a strong belief by the court that justice delayed is justice denied." People looking to the courts to solve a dispute make strategic legal decisions not based on the merits of their case or on fairness, but on what will cause their opponents enough delay to break them, or how they can avoid that delay themselves.

Selection

Judge Zouhary has another suggestion for improvement, one that relates to the judicial selection process. Ohio elects its state court judges in partisan elections. Judge Zouhary ran for a position on the state court and lost, but he gained enough prominence from campaign efforts and his courtroom career to be considered for a vacancy appointment to that same bench. At the same time, there was an opening on the federal bench. Judge Zouhary openly pursued both—and got both. He was appointed to the state court bench in March 2005 and then to federal court in April 2006. He is an example of a judge who has run the gauntlet of judicial selection methods: partisan election (he lost), vacancy appointment, and federal court appointment. He decries "the perception that judges are political creatures and they bring their politics to the bench, influencing the decisions they make." Rather, Judge Zouhary has not found that to be the case, "especially at the trial court level where I believe no matter who appoints you, the end result would be the same in the vast majority of cases—maybe 95 percent." Of selection methods, he notes:

> When I ran to be a state court judge, I wasn't studying law books to become a good judge. I was putting up signs and trying to get my name known because I was told there's only one thing that matters—and that is name recognition. So, there's a bit of a disjoint when you have election of judges—doing what you need to do to get elected judge has nothing to do with whether you'll be a good judge. And that's a difficult transition.

Judge Bennett chimes in on that point as well. He believes that judges should be appointed for life tenure after recommendation from merit-selected panels, but should also be evaluated along the way by colleagues, jurors, litigants, and lawyers to assure continuing accountability.

Jurors and Jury Trials

Judges Bennett and Zouhary are vocal supporters of the civil jury trial and have developed practices designed to support the jurors. Judge Zouhary vowed never to keep the jury waiting—and he doesn't. Posttrial evaluations from jurors give Judge Zouhary and his staff high marks, expressing near unanimous consent that their experience was better than expected. Judge Bennett runs jury trials from 8:30 AM to 2:30 PM with just two twenty minute breaks in the day, and he gives jurors stretch breaks every forty minutes. He presents voir dire, a preliminary examination to determine the competency of a witness or juror, using

PowerPoint, and gives each juror an individual set of complete jury instructions before opening statements in every trial. These instructions are in plain English and vetted by a focus group of former jurors from previous trials. They have a table of contents and a verdict chart form, which allows the jurors to see, in a visual snapshot, all the issues they will be asked to decide. He meets with the jury after the verdict, answers their questions, and then provides them with a form giving them an opportunity to critique him as their trial judge, the skill and ability of the lawyers, the trial process, the jury instructions, and the courthouse staff. The jurors are asked to take the form home, fill it out, and mail it back in a self-addressed stamped envelope. Judge Bennett says:

> Each innovation stemmed from a different inspiration, but my guiding principle, as a judge in a federal court that has led the nation in trials per judge in the last decade more often than any other of the ninety-four districts, is a jury-centered approach to judging. So I continuously ask myself, "What would I want if I were a juror in this court?"

State Court Judges—Same Song, Second Verse

The state trial court judges echo similar themes—though it is important to remember that the context and the caseload are quite different in the state courts. The grand, majestic federal courthouses around the nation are frequently empty. Their business is increasingly conducted by telephone and in chambers. The caseload is, by state court standards, light, and although there are clearly budget problems looming (including judicial salaries), the funding is still significantly better than at the state level. In sharp contrast, state courts see more than 100 million cases filed annually. The hallways are likely to be filled with jurors, crying infants, and prisoners in orange garb all at the same time; the dockets are jammed and the funding is plummeting. These are the courts where syndi-courts find their material and where citizens of all walks of life come for resolution of their issues.

But even with those differences, there are profound commonalities. Lael Montgomery and Henry Kantor are trial court judges in Colorado and Oregon, respectively. Judge Montgomery's courthouse backs up to the Flatiron rock formations in Boulder, and Judge Kantor's to the Willamette River in Portland. They have both been on the bench for more than a decade—Judge Montgomery from a prosecutor's office and Judge Kantor from a litigation practice primarily representing plaintiffs. Both were trial lawyers, and both did a stint in a limited jurisdiction court before taking their current positions.

For both of them, the question is how best to serve the end-users of the system. For example, when she was in county court, Judge Montgomery changed the layout of the courtroom. She noticed that in criminal cases, the witness might be only five feet from the defendant against whom he or she was testifying. She thought, *This is not right*, so she moved the tables and changed the configuration of the courtroom. Judge Montgomery notes that

> judges come out of the lawyer culture, and lawyers
> think the courthouse is their personal domain...
> The courtroom belongs to those scared parents

in the back row…[I]t all starts with mindfulness about the people who come in with their adrenaline through the roof out of fear and concern for what they're going through…Translating the silly talk—"subsequent to that" means "after"—is helpful to anyone who's in an uncomfortable situation, whether it's a frightened defendant or a dad who's terrified he's never going to see his kids again.

Judge Kantor agrees, and one of the places where he applies that mindfulness is in case management. He points to the professional malpractice docket in Portland, which moves smoothly and efficiently. In Judge Montgomery's and Judge Kantor's courts, everyone has firm trial dates and access to the judge for resolution of issues (even by e-mail).

There is one difference in Oregon. Remember the Oregon Rules of Civil Procedure, which are very different from the Federal Rules and their state analogues that most judges apply across the country? The Oregon rules require fact-based pleading and do not permit discovery or disclosure of experts. Judge Kantor says:

I'm a real believer in the fact that we had a group of lawyers and judges who in the '60s and '70s got together and said, "You know, we're watching how things are going out of control in every other part of this country, in the federal system, and we are going to be different. We are not going to do that." They put their feet down. And it worked! So we never got federalized. We resisted. And now interestingly the feds are studying us to see how come we're handling things so well.

Judge Kantor thinks things are moving along well in the Oregon courts, in comparison to other courts around the nation. He credits collegiality and points to Oregon as a paragon of lawyer/judge cooperation. He sees sharp distinctions in other parts of the country where "the lawyers don't get along," noting:

> The judges feel the need to slam punishments on them, and that just makes it worse, and there is a reduction of civility and collegiality. It's almost like it's an us-versus-them now. Lawyers versus judges—in too many parts of the country.

Judge Kantor calls it a "local confluence between judges and lawyers." He suggests the model that led to the different rules adopted in Oregon in the 1970s—collaboration for the benefit of the system. He says that the current problems will "sink us all" if we cannot figure out a way to cooperate and solve them.

The solutions to the crisis in the courts lie in "mindfulness" of the needs of the users, case management, local culture, and—certainly according to Judge Kantor—different rules.

Appellate Judges

Now we are going to reach up the court ladder into the appellate ranks of state courts, beginning with Chief Judge Janice Davidson of the Colorado Court of Appeals. Chief Judge Davidson serves on a court of twenty-two judges—an intermediate court that serves to handle appeals from the trial courts. Their docket is diverse and heavy. Judge Davidson served as a trial court judge for three years before being appointed to the Colorado Court of Appeals in 1988. She has been chief judge of that court since 2003, chosen by the chief justice with the support of her colleagues.

She worries about the system, saying:

> Think about discovery—the abuses. This isn't every lawyer. But the civil justice system is too expensive and too frightening. Remember the supposed Gypsy curse: "May you never be in a lawsuit in which you are *right*." It's who's got the money. And that's driving the system, which goes in *both* directions. It really drives me nuts. So whether you go to ADR and settle a case as a defendant because you don't want to risk all the costs, or you're a plaintiff and take so much less than you deserve because you don't want to be on the hook, I see it getting worse and worse. And it shouldn't be. We need to fix that.

Chief Judge Davidson is a believer that judicial leadership requires consensus building, not autocratic decision making. She notes that she has great colleagues and strong administrative help and is dependent upon both. Judicial collegiality is one of the keys to success, in her view. Within that model, Chief Judge Davidson has changed the face of her court.

A decade ago, it was a court of sixteen judges, each of whom were required to write ninety to one hundred written opinions per year, and appeals could languish up to two or three years. Now, the court consists of twenty-two judges, each judge is responsible for seventy to eighty opinions per year, and the timeframe from notice of appeal to opinion is more like ten to twelve months. She is very proud of a new rule permitting a certain kind of interlocutory appeal in civil cases to be expedited: "If you get an early, quick response from the appellate court in a complex case you can save hundreds of thousands of dollars."

Chief Judge Davidson also points to dependency and neglect cases where appeals have been streamlined and expedited. She notes that

> one of the greatest places of progress has come in the dependency and neglect cases, because the longer these things drag on, the worse for the young child who is trying to find a family and get stability...[W]e got expedited dependency and neglect cases down to a matter of months, so the kids know where they're going to be. That was a major accomplishment.

Justice Ming Chin spent two years on the Alameda County trial court before moving to the First District Court of Appeals in San Francisco and then, in 1996, to the California Supreme Court. So he has seen the system from many different perspectives and he, too, has some thoughts about the problems and the solutions.

The first problem he mentions is that too many cases are resolved outside the system. He thinks this is going to be hard to solve in the current climate of budget cutting, but that it must be addressed. His suggested solution: broader, more cost-effective access to the system.

Also of concern to Justice Chin is that most judges have only one kind of experience, and they "fumble around" on the bench until they get the whole picture. They may not understand business law or criminal law—they have had only criminal or civil experience. Paradoxically, more-experienced judges often are not sophisticated in the workings of the electronic age.

Justice Chin tells stories of judges who are not prepared to grapple with new technology, despite the efficiencies it might offer. Justice Chin sees the whole system going electronic and says everyone had better get on board. His solution is training.

Another problem area that worries Justice Chin is court staff and judge demeanor and attitudes. He talks about his own experience:

> I practiced law in counties throughout the state, and there were times when I entered the court, and you'd have thought I was the garbage man by the way we were treated by clerks, the staff, even sometimes by the judges. And I swore when I got onto the bench that would never happen in my courtroom. The first thing I did was to sit down every member of my staff and say everyone who comes into this court will be treated with dignity and respect, whether you've had conflicts with them in the past or not. They took that to heart, because I started getting comments from lawyers asking me, "Where did you get your staff? Nobody in this courthouse treats us like this."

In this case, Justice Chin thinks performance evaluation for judges is one of the answers:

> Everybody knows which judges need to temper their "judge-itis" attitudes. But judicial performance evaluation can really help. Of course, it's often apples and oranges. A family judge might have fifty matters in a morning, whereas a judge with any kind of a complicated docket might only see two or three lawyers over a long time. You still need to do

it, though…and, the rise of anonymous juror questionnaires has been a great development. That's why anonymity was important, because a respondent may need to say, "Who does this judge think he is?"

Finally we turn to Chief Justice Wallace Jefferson in Texas. Chief Justice Jefferson practiced appellate law in Texas, arguing two cases before the US Supreme Court by the age of thirty-five and was appointed to the Texas Supreme Court in 2001. He was elected to that office in 2002, and in 2004 Governor Rick Perry promoted him to chief justice. In 2008, he was reelected to office.

Chief Justice Jefferson has two goals for his tenure on the court, the first of which is bringing national attention to the method of judicial selection in place in Texas and across the country. He states:

We read every day about the political affiliation of judges. Many want judges only from "our" party, but that is not what I believe. Judges must have courage to disregard politics, monetary contributions, criticism, or praise when deciding cases. The vast majority of our judges exhibit such courage routinely. Yet there is a perception, fueled by partisan campaigns, that Texas judges decide cases based not on the rule of law, but because they have the support of a political party or interest group. It is not true, but perception sometimes prevails over reality. And while Texans cherish their right to vote, it has become clear that in judicial elections, the public (particularly in large urban areas) cannot cast informed votes due to the sheer number of candidates on the ballot. This unfortunate

fact gives rise to occasional partisan sweeps of the
judiciary. When it happens, judges are elected
based not on merit or experience, but because their
political party has managed to prevail. This is a
strange way to select those who guard our legal
rights...I hope that we can recommend reforms so
that a vote for a judicial candidate is closely cor-
related with merit rather than political affiliation
or other irrelevant factors.

Chief Justice Jefferson's second goal is to advance
the transparency and effectiveness of the court. Under
his tenure, the Texas Supreme Court broadcasts oral
arguments live and archives them with the briefs on
the supreme court's website. He has also created a permanent commission on children, youth, and families
to expedite the process by which children removed
from the home through no fault of their own can be
swiftly reunited with their families or, where appropriate, placed in permanent adoptive homes.

These nine judges are problem solvers. They see real
problems with the way cases are managed; with costs
and delays within the system; with lack of attention to
the public's needs; with diminishing focus on jury trials
and jurors; and with judicial selection. But all of them,
in their particular courts, are devising solutions and
implementing those solutions. They are, as Judge Montgomery would say, mindful of the need to do things differently, and they are intent upon rebuilding justice.

The Court Administrators

These nine judges cannot do it alone, however. They
need the support of their colleagues and of the lawyers
and citizens of our nation. They also need the day-to-day

partnerships with administrators, the operations officers of the courts. (The function of court administration is actually a new profession, comparatively speaking.)

Sue Dosal, state court administrator in Minnesota, narrates the history of her field as follows:

> The profession borrowed heavily from hospital administration, recognizing that judges, like doctors, are fiercely independent but have to work within a system. Ernie Friesen started the Institute for Court Management at the University of Denver in 1970, occasioned by Chief Justice Burger's interest in improving the administration of justice and bringing modern business practices to the judiciary. ICM taught people how courts operate and how to be court administrators. It attracted people in midcareer—from business, law, and government—to become a cadre from which the federal and state courts could choose circuit executives and court administrators...This was part of a national movement in structural and administrative reform, in part because of a litigation explosion.

Dosal talks about her role as "essentially the CEO for the Minnesota Judicial Branch" (315 judges, 2,500 employees, 99 locations, $285 million annually), in which she works for the judicial council chaired by the chief justice (which Dosal views as akin to her board of directors). Also, her office provides central infrastructure services, human resources, finance, legal research, technology, and evaluation, and it serves as the branch's liaison to the executive and legislative branches, working with them to get the judiciary the funding it needs to do its job.

Dosal has seen it all. When she began, there were no computers—only big leather-bound books with court records in them. Now, the Minnesota courts handle 1.7 million cases per year and have a single statewide technology—a Web-based system covering all courts.

The courts have undergone many fundamental changes over the last thirty years, according to Dosal. First, they have undergone structural change: levels of courts were combined from many courts into one trial court that is more flexible and less duplicative. Intermediate courts of appeal were created in a number of states to allow a more streamlined, efficient handling of cases. Funding models were changed as well, from local to statewide.

And now she is moving into the next phase:

In 2008, our Judicial Council created the Access and Service Delivery Committee to deal with these new cost pressures in what we call the "new normal." Essentially, we're talking about leveraging technology, streamlining workflow, and taking a look at lower-cost subordinate judicial officers to do some of the work that we now do. We've been working at a very fast pace on this. As an example, we have looked at all of our cases, and out of the 1.7 million cases about 1 million are what we call "payable citations." We are now in the process of transitioning those one million from their eighty-seven different locations into a unified virtual payment center with fewer, lower-paid employees working from their homes to support citation entry and a statewide call center. Payments can be made 24/7 online or by automated telephone system. Overdue debt is automatically referred to our collections vendor. All of this improves customer service, reduces processing costs, and increases revenue to state and local government.

The devil that plagues Dosal is budget woes. She explains:

> The state has a $6.2 billion deficit, which amounts to 18 percent of our [state] budget. And it's not a short-term problem, with the demographic shifts of baby boomers retiring and needing more services even as their tax receipts decline by 50 percent after they retire. We have lost 10 percent of our staff statewide, and if we don't innovate, we'll actually have to stop handling some kinds of cases. So stage three is thinking outside the silos and finding ways to redesign and innovate service delivery.

Dosal recognizes that public trust and confidence are "what we live and die by, particularly now, when there's not enough money to go around." Dosal's perspective is a thoughtful one:

> Everyone needs to see that we're doing everything we can to maximize service efficiency *and* effectiveness with limited means. We're trying to be ahead of the curve, to look at it from a taxpayer's standpoint. Which is why I always try to ask myself what my neighbors would say…That's our lens.

That lens of the user, the ultimate beneficiary of the court service, is the same lens that Marcus Reinkensmeyer applies to his work as court administrator for the Judicial Branch of Arizona in Maricopa County.

In 2002, he became the senior executive officer for
the judicial branch. His budget is about $232 million,
with 3,600 staff members—after the last cutbacks—
and probably fifty buildings, all with the accompanying concerns related to security, technology, logistics,
and infrastructure.

He focuses on public service and access:

> Public access has been first—using technology. We
> were one of the first jurisdictions to put our docket
> online, and online case lookup, meaning our web-
> site is more than a public relations exercise. Forms
> and navigational tools, plus the self-service center
> that was originally set up for self-represented liti-
> gants, are actually being used by attorneys too now.
> We have more than eight hundred forms on there,
> all of which have made the whole system more
> affordable and manageable. You can arrive at the
> court much better prepared to navigate the system.

He sees seismic shifts in the way courts operate
and perceive themselves:

> For years, the courts were run according to mys-
> terious, esoteric rules written by attorneys and
> professors, and it almost amounted to a kind of
> insider training. The last decade has seen a huge
> transformation toward making the system user-
> friendly and understandable to public, for both
> represented and self-represented litigants.

Like Dosal, Reinkensmeyer is very worried about
budgets: "The last couple of years we lost about 420
positions and $20 million...Plus no pay raises, fewer

promotional opportunities, and people working longer hours on top of that." But he never loses sight of his primary goal; he guides himself and his organization along an axis of "What can we do to serve you better?"

Melinda Taylor, district administrator to the 17th Judicial District in Colorado, is also passionate about customer service. Her court has developed positions designed to bridge the gap between the courts, social services, and medical services for families in need—better for the users, and better for the judges. They have a pool of employees by case type who float throughout the building to wherever help is most needed, in order to permit cross-training, team building, and efficiency. They also have an early neutral assessment program, which is a "male-female team that screens domestic relations cases for judges." Rather than mediating or investigating, this team helps "parents realize that they want to cooperate to get through this for themselves and their children."

They have a new self-help center, which is "more than a magazine rack with forms." Chief Judge Vincent Phelps, along with Taylor and the local bar association are working to ensure that it is really a functioning center that makes the system more navigable.

And Taylor is a proponent of active case management. Her district is implementing a differentiated case management system that insures consistent case-appropriate attention from a judge through the life of the case. She says:

> It's a well-known statistic among our judges and people familiar with case management that 3 percent of our cases require most of our attention. I think we need to learn to drill down better into

those few cases and deal with the 97 percent remainder efficiently and with high quality.

Lastly, Taylor sees the budget crisis too, but is trying to stay positive. She challenges the leaders at all levels in the system to be realistically creative, to come into the same room, and commit to a common vision—and then go do it.

There *is* a common vision emerging out of the hard reality that the system is indeed in crisis, in danger of becoming irrelevant, and on the brink of losing public trust and confidence. The vision is a new lens, a new mindfulness, a new focus—the needs of the users of the system.

10

Building Citizen-Centered Courts

Judge Kevin Burke of Minnesota asks why the courts cannot be like Neiman Marcus—committed to customer service. He's got a good point. The civil courts exist to serve citizens: parties to current lawsuits, parties to lawsuits to come, witnesses, and jurors. They exist to serve the rule of law, which, in turn, benefits each of us. Why are citizens not then at the center of every equation, every decision?

Let's posit a twenty-first-century courthouse that is user-friendly in every sense: the building, the signage and ease of navigation, the online explanations, rules and forms. That courthouse, both real and virtual, should be somewhere people can go to resolve their disputes and enforce their rights as efficiently and fairly as possible. Concierges or receptionists or intake personnel should guide people to the service they need. Basic legal advice should be available as well as referrals to lawyers for those who need representation.

Once we enter the courtroom itself, imagine a place where the judge is highly capable, fair, efficient, and well respected. Imagine a courtroom where the record is kept electronically, files are electronically accessible, and the public is welcome. Imagine transparency and trustworthiness. Imagine a place where individuals, businesses, and government entities all trust that their cases will be heard promptly and decided justly.

We all have not just a role but a responsibility in helping to achieve these outcomes, whether we're citizens, court staff, legislators, lawyers, or judges. First, as citizens we must value the courts, learn about them, and follow their successes and failures. Courts are every bit as important to our way of life as the executive or legislative branches, but they are widely ignored and misunderstood. Civics education for middle and high school students is only part of the answer; the other part must be an understanding by adults that courts matter and they cannot be taken for granted.

Legislatures and Congress must fund the courts adequately, but we the people must support such funding efforts vigorously. Courts are an easy target for budget cutting, because they do not have an obvious, compelling constituency to plead their cause. So, we all have to be that constituency.

As citizens, we must appreciate and protect the right to a jury trial. Juries do not deserve the bad press they have received. On the contrary, they are a foundational part of our system: the ultimate opportunity to inject community standards and common sense into the justice system. In almost all cases, jury trials benefit the litigants, the jurors, and the system. Lawsuits spinning out of control in the pretrial process and ultimately disgorging settlements born of exhaustion do not benefit anyone. We must strip away the impediments to jury trials and provide jurors with the tools to make good decisions.

Finally, we must take great care not to let politics infect the process of choosing and evaluating judges.

When a judge appears to have been influenced by a political party, ideology, or campaign donor, the rule of law is at risk. When Americans see judges as yet another breed of politician, beholden to those who support them, they lose confidence in the courts as a safe place where equal justice under law prevails. When society moves in that direction, we put democracy in jeopardy. No longer do we have a viable system of checks and balances.

So imagine instead a selection system that identifies judicial candidates on the basis of legal skill, experience, and capacity to be impartial. Imagine a system that seats those judges and then measures and evaluates them to assure that they are impartial, attentive, and enforcing the rule of law. As citizens, we can help make this happen too—through the O'Connor Judicial Selection Plan that includes the vetting of candidates by an open, transparent, and balanced nominating process described earlier in this book.

As for lawyers and judges, our duty is the highest and the most difficult. We need to be thoughtful, bold, innovative, and collaborative. We need to begin with the premise that the system is fundamentally sound, but in need of significant reform—which is possible. The civil rules committees and judges who are in charge of writing the rules of the civil justice system need to remember why they went to law school in the first place. It was likely *not* to argue or resolve discovery motions or sort through e-mails—it was to serve justice. They need to take a fresh look at the civil justice system, including the rules of civil procedure, and restructure it to ensure efficient, affordable handling of cases. We can't allow the system to be captive to process, more process, and yet more process. Delay and gamesmanship cripple litigants financially and destroy confidence in a just system. The rules and other court procedures need to be recalibrated to identify the issues at an early point in time, mandate the exchange of information between the parties, target specific discovery, and move the case to trial. If at some point the parties themselves choose to settle their case because they have learned something that impacts their decision about ultimate outcome, that is perfectly appropriate. But the system itself should not be built around forcing settlements. We need twenty-first-century procedures for twenty-first-century lawsuits.

Additionally, we need to ask judges to manage cases actively (and reward them in their performance evaluations when they do). Judges should apply business concepts of efficiency and project management to case processing, and plan for explosions in the use of technology. All court systems should permit electronic filing, permit telephonic or videoconferencing hearings, and begin to consider how to maximize technology for the benefit of the litigants in the system. Listening to businesspeople and technology experts is one place to begin; we have historically listened only to judges and lawyers.

Before we can be open to change, we all need to step out of our respective boxes. Plaintiffs' lawyers, defense lawyers, corporate counsel, and judges (and the rest of us, for that matter) all tend toward polarity, defensiveness, and myopia when critiqued. The result has been change paralysis. We zero each other out with the quibbles and finger-pointing and resistance to change. Meanwhile, litigants are horrified by the system we have built, and the American public is the ultimate loser.

We must not sacrifice the good on the altar of the perfect. Lawyers and judges in particular have been trained to anticipate every possible eventuality, and they design systems that accommodate that outlook. The result is a byzantine complex that is intended to serve everyone but actually serves almost no one. So design the system for the 80 percent, and provide alternatives for the 20 percent who need to be treated differently. Designing a system for 20 percent of cases guarantees overkill.

All of this vision is not merely possible, parts of it already exist in various places around the country. The judges, the court staff, and the administrators who understand that perspective are building out their courts accordingly. We have introduced you to some of those individuals in previous chapters, but there are countless others. For example, management at Nike went to the chief justice of Oregon and asked if the Oregon courts could create a pilot project in which civil cases would be able to get to trial (with limited discovery) in four months. Nike management said that, if this were done, Nike would consider diverting its cases back to the courts instead of into arbitration. The chief justice created such a program, and it is now operating. *That* is accountability and relevance. Both individuals deserve applause.

Arizona and Utah courts now host websites that provide information about the court's ratings on a measurement system designed by the National Center for State Courts. In one jurisdiction, the website shows a dashboard and indicates where the court comes out on the various dials. Those jurisdictions deserve applause. In Indiana, the courts are besieged with foreclosures. The Indiana legislature enacted a law providing that the courts could allow the parties to mediate the dispute. The notice of the mediation option was sandwiched into the papers being sent out to debtors, and no one paid any attention. The court itself decided to send out a separate notice to the parties, and, lo and behold, people began opting for mediation; an Indiana clerk reports that they are resolving 40 percent of the foreclosure actions in her court in a way that allows the debtor to retain the home and figure out a workable payment schedule. That is a court that is citizen-centric.

Our vision is simple: courts that are built for service to the public. Remember the "cattle call" docket that benefited no one but the judge? In our vision, that would never happen in any courtroom in the country. Rather, every procedure would be designed for the person or party seeking justice: to facilitate just, speedy, and inexpensive access to an impartial judge and to a jury when appropriate. When courts work to implement this vision, the citizenry must in turn support and value them. Courts are not expendable; they are vital. Of all the institutions that support our way of life, they are perhaps the most vital. We cannot afford to allow them to wither. Individually and collectively, let each of us begin *now* to do our part.

Primer
Courts and Lawsuits 101

F or those who haven't spent as much time in courthouses as we have, it might help to review some of
the basics of courts and lawsuits. By basics we mean
both the basics of civic education that are so fundamentally lacking in our society today and also the
basics of this book, some of which might be unfamiliar even to those who walk the courthouse halls daily.
Readers new to the court system are encouraged to
refer to the glossary, tables, and endnotes for further
detail on the process and structure of the system.

The Real Basics
We live in a republic, not a democracy. The difference is important, particularly when discussing the
courts. We have a constitution that grants to government only those powers necessary to secure the rights
of the individual. We have three branches of government, designed to counterbalance one another and to
prevent even the majority from overtaking the individual's rights. As stated by Hamilton Abert Long:

> The American philosophy and system of govern-
> ment thus bar equally the "snob-rule" of a govern-
> ing Elite and the "mob-rule" of an Omnipotent

Majority. This is designed, above all else, to preclude the existence in America of any governmental power capable of being misused so as to violate The Individual's rights—to endanger the people's liberties.[1]

Hence, the vitality of a strong third leg of the stool is critical to the appropriate functioning of the other two. Without strong courts, either the executive or the legislative branch of government can hold too much sway, to the detriment of individual rights.

The third branch of government is composed of the courts. This is true at both the state and federal levels: there is at least one federal court in every state, as well as state and oftentimes municipal courts. Constitutions and statutes embody the law, but, these courts apply the law. Should these courts cease to function well, we will have no rule of law and no promise of justice.

The courts hear two basic kinds of cases: criminal and civil. Criminal cases are those in which a defendant is being prosecuted by the government for a crime and is facing punishment, which might include the loss of liberty. Civil cases—the focus of this book—are those in which two or more parties have a dispute and in which compensation for the injured party usually involves the payment of money. Significantly more Americans will encounter the civil justice system than will have contact with the criminal justice system (perhaps excluding minor traffic offenses). If you hit someone with your car, or someone hits you; if you have a disagreement with your business partner or the roofer you hired to fix your roof; if your home is being foreclosed upon; if you have a dispute with your landlord over a lease, or if you are a landlord and have a dispute with your tenant; if you believe you were wrongfully terminated from a job, or someone claims you wrongfully terminated them; if you get divorced—in all of these instances, you will come in contact with the civil justice system. In short, our livelihoods, homes, children, marriages, and bank accounts all can be at issue in civil cases in this country's courts.

Although similar in certain ways, such as many of the rules and procedures under which they operate, the courts at the state and federal level are in fact quite different because of the nature of the cases—civil and criminal—they are designed to handle and the method by which their judges are chosen. Let us take each in turn.

The Structure

The federal system is composed of one or more federal district (and bankruptcy) courts in each state, courts of appeals, and the US Supreme Court. The federal district courts are trial courts, handling both civil and criminal (but almost never family) matters. These courts have jurisdiction over criminal cases and three general types of civil jurisdiction. "Federal question jurisdiction" arises when a party seeks relief under a federal law or the US Constitution—for example, regulation of interstate commerce, allegations of unfair competition, patents, copyrights, IRS matters, civil rights, Indian matters, and others. (Each federal district court also has a special unit, a separate bankruptcy court for those cases.) "Diversity jurisdiction" permits a citizen of one state to sue a citizen of another state on a matter of state law if the amount at issue is at least $75,000. Finally, through "supplemental" or "ancillary" jurisdiction, the federal courts may exercise jurisdiction over a claim based on state law when it arises in a case that also has a federal claim.

An appeal from a federal district court is to a court of appeals (appellate court) whose function is to review what happened in the trial court and determine whether the district judge made errors in his or her rulings on the law or procedure. The processes employed are similar to those in appellate courts at the state level: the filing of briefs and, in some cases, oral presentations by the parties and written opinions by the judges explaining their decision. Most appellate courts do their work through randomly selected panels of judges. There is a court of appeals in each of the twelve regional federal judicial circuits (including the District of Columbia) and a federal circuit (whose court of appeals has a national jurisdiction over certain types of cases, mainly those involving patents). Circuits include clusters of states or US territories. For example, the Ninth Circuit covers Alaska, Arizona, California, Idaho, Montana, Nevada, Oregon, Washington, Guam, the Northern Mariana Islands, and Hawaii. The Second Circuit covers Connecticut, New York, and Vermont.

In addition to the federal district and bankruptcy courts and courts of appeals, the federal court system includes a few specialized courts, such as the Court of International Trade, which hears cases involving particular trade and customs laws. There are also courts in the executive branch of government, such as the US Tax Court, immigration courts, and courts for the armed services.

Recourse from the courts of appeals (or, for some cases, state supreme courts) is to the US Supreme

Court. A losing party (the appellant) seeking to overturn the lower court's decision petitions the Court to take the case, through a petition for writ of certiorari (commonly referred to as a "cert petition"). The Court denies almost all petitions. Of more than eight thousand filed each year, the justices agree to decide less than one hundred in which they hear oral arguments from the parties' lawyers and issue full opinions explaining their decisions. They write orders for another fifty to sixty without oral argument. The US Supreme Court estimates that each justice generates approximately five thousand pages of written opinions each term.

The federal courts' caseload is dwarfed by that of the state court system. In addition to the caseload of the US Supreme Court, 282,307 civil and 77,287 criminal cases were commenced in federal district courts and 56,790 appeals were filed with the courts of appeals in 2010.[2] By contrast, in 2008 a record 106 million cases were filed—of those, 19.4 million were civil cases and 5.7 million were domestic relations cases.[3] State court is where the action is.

The state court system parallels the federal system in part, with each state having a general jurisdiction trial court, most states (but not all) having an intermediate appellate court, and all states having at least one court of last resort, usually called a supreme court. The general jurisdiction trial courts usually handle felony criminal matters, divorces, probate, and juvenile matters, and civil cases seeking damages over a certain amount. There are other levels of trial courts— sometimes folded in with the general jurisdiction court and sometimes separated out—that handle traffic offenses, more minor criminal matters, landlord/

tenant disputes, and civil cases with lower financial amounts in dispute. Larger municipalities have their own courts as well, which handle traffic infractions and ordinance violations. Cases move through this system in a similar manner as in the federal system, with the bulk of appeals handled by the intermediate appellate courts of appeals and review by the state supreme courts by cert petition, and at the discretion of the court, although some states are exceptions to this general description.

Civil cases may also move between the state and federal system. If a case is filed in state court that could have been filed in federal court, one of the parties might seek to transfer ("remove") it to the federal system. Similarly, a federal district court can send ("remand") all or a portion of a case to the state court as appropriate.

The Lawsuit

Now that the basic diagram of the judicial system itself is in place, we turn to the specific workings of a lawsuit. For readers unfamiliar with the civil court system, understanding how a civil lawsuit works in principle is important when we start talking about rules and case management. The description that follows is also important for those of us who make our living in the courtroom, as it illustrates the simplicity with which the process was intended to work, but often does not.

The process begins with a plaintiff filing a complaint, which the defendant must either answer or move to dismiss (if the judge denies that motion then the defendant files an answer). The case is then "at issue." Generally, what happens next is that the parties start into the discovery phase of the lawsuit, either with court oversight or without, depending upon the rules and the process for that court.

Discovery usually involves some combination of the following tools:

- Interrogatories—posing written questions to the other side
- Requests for admission—written requests for the other side to admit certain facts
- Depositions—in-person oral examinations with a court reporter (stenographer) and/or a videographer in which the opposing attorney asks questions of the deponent or witness
- Requests for production of documents—requests that the other side compile and produce all documents responsive to identified categories

This phase can take anywhere from two months to years; it can involve two depositions or dozens; it can implicate a hundred written documents or millions of electronically stored documents.

At some point in the pretrial process, a judge might become involved and will hold a conference for the purpose of getting a handle on the scope of the case, the issues, and the logistics. In some courts, trial dates are set at an early point; in others, they are not set unless the case actually appears to be headed for trial.

If one of the parties believes that the facts and law of the case are undisputed as to one or more claims, that party can seek to resolve the case before trial by filing a motion for summary judgment. The judge will then review the law, affidavits, and/or discovery excerpts setting forth the facts, and decide whether there is a contested issue of material fact warranting a trial. If there is not, summary judgment can enter and the case is over at the trial level. If there are contested facts, then the case moves on toward trial. So far, all of the proceedings in the case have most likely taken place on paper, on the telephone, or in the judge's office (chambers). The case has likely not seen the light of a courtroom.

In principle, the chart on the following page illustrates how the pretrial process is designed to proceed in the simplest federal civil case involving only two parties and assuming the longest time period allowed under the rules.

However, in practice, even under the simplest situation imaginable, it can be far more complicated.

The second chart, on page 202, even on cursory examination, demonstrates that the process has spun far afield from its original intended course.

At some point in the pretrial process, the judge is likely to require or at least suggest that the parties take their dispute to some form of alternative dispute resolution (ADR), which can mean presenting the dispute to a mediator or perhaps a panel of arbitrators. (Congress has told federal courts that they must at least offer all parties in a civil dispute some form of ADR.) In some courts, the arbitrators' decision is final, which means that the case is over, though there might have been serious errors in the process from which there is no recourse. Or parties might go through some form of mediation, which is a process designed to identify the underlying cause of the dispute and perhaps produce a resolution. There are also a couple of other options afoot that bear description. Some states in the country permit what is called "private judging," or more

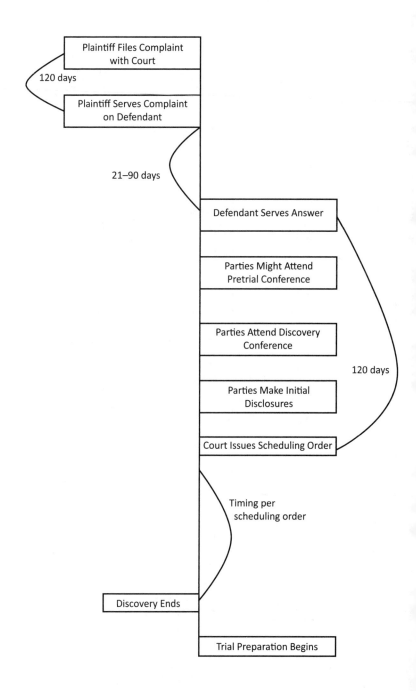

Plaintiff Files Complaint
with Court

120 days

Plaintiff Serves Complaint
on Defendant

21–90 days

Defendant Serves Answer

Parties Might Attend
Pretrial Conference

Parties Attend Discovery
Conference

120 days

Parties Make Initial
Disclosures

Court Issues Scheduling Order

Timing per
scheduling order

Discovery Ends

Trial Preparation Begins

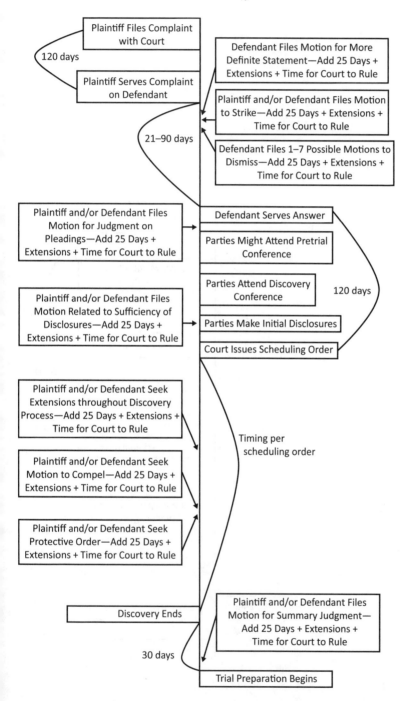

colloquially, "rent-a-judge." In that process, the parties chose a retired judge to handle the case. That judge is paid, but otherwise handles the case as if it were in the system. The procedural rules apply, hearings are on the record, and there is even access to a jury trial if the parties wish to go that way. The appropriateness of ADR as a goal of the court system is something we questioned in earlier chapters. Suffice it to say here that ADR is falling out of favor with some because it too has become too complex and too expensive.

This, then, is the basic schematic of the courts and lawsuits.

Endnotes

1. Civics and the Courts: A Crisis Hidden in Plain View

1. "Sen. Schumer on the Three Branches of Government," YouTube video, 1:26, from an interview televised by CNN on January 30, 2011, posted by "thebcast," January 30, 2011, www.youtube.com /watch?v=fG0Jpu9geWY.

2. "Startling Lack of Constitutional Knowledge Revealed in First-Ever National Poll," National Constitution Center, http://ratify .constitutioncenter.org/CitizenAction/CivicResearchResults/ NCCNationalPoll/Index.shtml (accessed March 14, 2011); "NCC National Poll: Highlights of Survey," National Constitution Center, http://ratify.constitutioncenter.org/CitizenAction /CivicResearchResults/NCCNationalPoll/HighlightsofthePoll .shtml (accessed March 14, 2011).

3. Ibid.

4. "NCC Teens' Poll: New Survey Shows Wide Gap Between Teens' Knowledge of Constitution and Knowledge of Pop Culture," National Constitution Center, http://ratify.constitutioncenter.org /CitizenAction/CivicResearchResults/NCCTeens%27Poll.shtml (accessed March 14, 2011).

5. Ibid.

6. Ibid.

7. Ibid.

8. Kimberlianne Podlas, "Blame Judge Judy: The Effects of Syndicated Television Courtrooms on Jurors," *American Journal of Trial Advocacy* 25 (2002): 557.

9. Ibid., 557.

10. Ibid., 566–567.

11. Hon. Bruce M. Selya, "The Confidence Game: Public Perceptions of the Judiciary," *New England Law Review* 30 (1996): 909, 912.

12. Annenberg Public Policy Center, *2007 Annenberg Public Policy Center Judicial Survey Results,* October 17, 2007, available at www

.law.georgetown.edu/judiciary/documents/finalversionJUDICIAL
FINDINGSoct1707.pdf.

13. Ibid.

14. "Our Fading Heritage: Americans Fail a Basic Test on Their History and Institutions—Television—Including TV News—Dumbs America Down," Intercollegiate Studies Institute, www.american civicliteracy.org/2008/major_findings_finding4.html (accessed March 14, 2011).

15. "Our Fading Heritage: Americans Fail a Basic Test on Their History and Institutions—Report Card," Intercollegiate Studies Institute, www.americancivicliteracy.org/2008/report_card.html (accessed March 14, 2011).

16. *TheLedger.com*, "U.S. Constitution: A Reading Assignment," editorial, September 17, 2010, www.theledger.com/article/20100917 /EDIT01/9165078.

17. Ibid.

18. "Our Fading Heritage: Americans Fail a Basic Test on Their History and Institutions—Major Findings: Finding 1: Americans Fail the Test of Civil Literacy," Intercollegiate Studies Institute, www .americancivicliteracy.org/2008/major_findings_finding1.html (accessed March 14, 2011).

19. Ibid.

20. "Our Fading Heritage: Americans Fail a Basic Test on Their History and Institutions—Additional Findings," Intercollegiate Studies Institute, www.americancivicliteracy.org/2008/additional _finding.html (accessed March 14, 2011).

21. Pete Winn, "Americans Know 'American Idol' Star Better than American History," *CNSNews.com*, November 20, 2008, www .cnsnews.com/news/article/39715 (discussing Bunting's 2008 address to the National Press Club).

22. "Our Fading Heritage: Americans Fail a Basic Test on Their History and Institutions—Major Findings: Finding 3: College Adds Little to Civic Knowledge," Intercollegiate Studies Institute, www.americancivicliteracy.org/2008/major_findings_finding3. html (accessed March 14, 2011).

23. Winn, "Americans Know 'American Idol' Star Better than American History," November 20, 2008.

24. Ibid.

25. Matthew Ladner, Goldwater Institute, "Freedom From Responsibility: A Survey of Civil Knowledge Among Arizona High School Students," *Policy Brief* No. 09-04 (June 30, 2009).

26. Ibid., 12–13.

27. Ibid., 3.

28. James L. Gibson and Gregory A. Caldeira, "Knowing the Supreme Court? A Reconsideration of Public Ignorance of the High Court," *Journal of Politics* 71 (2009): 429.

29. Ibid., 430.

30. James L. Gibson, "Public Images and Understandings of Courts" in *The Oxford Handbook of Empirical Legal Research*, ed. Peter Cane and Herbert M. Kritzer (Oxford: Oxford Univ. Press, 2010), 836.

31. Ibid., 836–37.

32. Ibid., 837.

33. David H. Souter, retired associate justice of the Supreme Court of the US, "Make American Civic Education Real Again" (address, American Bar Association Annual Meeting opening assembly, Chicago, August 1, 2009), www.abanow.org/2009/08/souter-tells -aba-annual-meeting-opening-assembly-that-civic-education-is-critical-to-preserving-an-independent-judiciary.

34. Ibid.

35. Mary Ellen Flannery and Karen Zauber, "Courting Kids: An Interview with Sandra Day O'Connor," *NEA Today*, March 2010, www.nea.org/home/38146.htm.

36. Linda Valdez, "Lassoing Young Minds," *Arizona Republic*, August 2, 2009.

37. Ibid.

38. Jon Stewart, "Behind the Robes," *The Daily Show with Jon Stewart* video, 4:59, March 3, 2009, www.comedycentral.com/videos/ index.jhtml?videoId=220242&title=sandra-day-o-connor-pt--1.

39. Jonathan Saltzman, "Off the Bench, Judge Blogs Her Mind; Gertner's Observations an Anomaly in Mass.," *Boston Globe*, May 27, 2008.

40. A Colorado Judicial Institute/Colorado Bar Association project, spearheaded by Russell Carparelli, a Colorado Court of Appeals judge and Marcia Krieger, a Colorado federal district court judge.

2. Gambling on Judges

1. Alexander Hamilton, "The Federalist No. 78: The Judiciary Department," *Independent Journal* (June 14, 1788).

2. Chief Justice John Roberts, *2010 Year-End Report on the Federal Judiciary* (December 31, 2010): 7–8, www.supremecourt.gov/public info/year-end/year-endreports.aspx.

3. Steven M. Puiszis, ed., *Without Fear or Favor in 2011: A New Decade of Challenges to Judicial Independence and Accountability* (Chicago: DRI, 2011), 72.

4. American Bar Association, *Report to the House of Delegates*, Res. 118.

5. Mark Sherman, "ABA Seeks to Reduce Bipartisan Fight on

Judges," Associated Press, August 11, 2008.

6. Russell Wheeler and Rebecca Love Kourlis, Options for Federal Judicial Screening Committees: Things to Consider in Establishing and Operating a Committee to Advise Legislators about Candidates for District Judgeships (and Other Judicial System Positions) (Washington, DC: Governance Institute, 2010, and Denver: Institute for the Advancement of the American Legal System, 2010), 2; Puiszis, *Without Fear or Favor in 2011*, 72.

7. See, e.g., The Brookings Institution, Breaking the Judicial Nominations and Confirmations Logjam, "Panel Two—Prospects for Change: Reforming Senate Rules Surrounding Confirmation" (uncorrected transcript, February 28, 2011), 6, available at www .brookings.edu/events/2011/0228_judicial_logjam.aspx (detailing a suggestion made by Eleanor Acheson).

8. Roscoe Pound, "The Causes of Popular Dissatisfaction with the Administration of Justice" (lecture, American Bar Association Annual Meeting, St. Paul, Minnesota, August 29, 1906); Richard B. Allen, ed., "Roscoe Pound Kindles the Spark of Reform," *American Bar Association Journal* 57 (April 1971): 348–351.

9. John Grisham, *The Appeal* (New York: Random House, Inc., 2008), 82-83. Note that the statistics cited by Grisham regarding number of states who elect appellate and supreme court judges is inaccurate. Only twenty-two states do so.

10. Buchanan, Ingersoll & Rooney PC and Harman Development Corporation, press release, May 15, 2008, www.brennancenter .org/page/-/Democracy/05-20-08%20Olson%20Press%20 Release.pdf.

11. *Caperton v. A. T. Massey Coal Co.*, 129 S. Ct. 2252 (June 8, 2009).

12. William W. Crowdus, "Twenty Years of the Missouri Nonpartisan Court Plan," *Journal of the Missouri Bar* 66 (July-August 2010): 210. Previously published as "Twenty Years of the Missouri Nonpartisan Court Plan," *Journal of the Missouri Bar* (1962) and (1976).

13. Ibid., 211.

14. Ibid.

15. Gregory J. Hobbs Jr., "Colorado Judicial Merit Selection—A Well-Deserved 40th Anniversary Celebration," *Colorado Lawyer* 35 (April 2006): 16.

16. Ibid.

17. Henry Kantor, interview by Dirk Olin, February 13, 2010.

18. *Republican Party of Minnesota v. White*, 536 U.S. 765, 787 (2002).

19. "The Florida Family Policy Council's 2008 Statewide Judicial Candidate Questionnaire," Florida Family Policy Council, www .judicialcampaignoversight.org/resourcecenter/committee-activities

/monitoring/pdfs/FFPC_Judges_2008_sm.pdf (accessed March 14, 2011).

20. Charles Hall, ed., *The New Politics of Judicial Elections 2000-2009: Decade of Change* (Washington, DC: Justice at Stake, 2010), 1.

21. Clint Brewer and Grant Schulte, "Influence of Special Interests Felt in State Courts," *USA Today*, January 28, 2011, www.usatoday.com/news/nation/2011-01-28-iowasupreme28_ST_N.htm.

22. "Judicial Elections 2010: TV Spending Surges in State Supreme Court Races," Justice at Stake, October 29, 2010, www.justiceatstake.org/state/judicial_elections_2010/election_2010_news_releases.cfm/judicial_elections_2010_tv_spending_surges?show=news&newsID=9104 (accessed March 14, 2011); "Judicial Elections 2010: 2010 Judicial Elections Increase Pressure on Courts, Reform Groups Say," Justice at Stake, November 3, 2010, www.justiceatstake.org/state/judicial_elections_2010/election_2010_news_releases.cfm/2010_judicial_elections_increase_pressure_on_courts_reform_groups_say?show=news&newsID=9129 (accessed March 14, 2011).

23. Ibid.

24. Ibid.

25. Rebecca Love Kourlis (speech, 2010 Kiroff Bench/Bar Conference, Toledo, Ohio, October 29, 2010).

26. Jesse Rutledge, ed., *The New Politics of Judicial Elections 2006*, "2010 Judicial Elections Increase Pressure on Courts, Reform Groups Say," Justice at Stake, November 3, 2010, vi; Deborah Goldberg, Craig Holman, and Samantha Sanchez, *The New Politics of Judicial Elections* (2002), 5.

27. Rutledge, *The New Politics of Judicial Elections 2006*, vi.

28. Quoted in Adam Liptak, "American Exceptionalism: Rendering Justice, With One Eye on Re-election," *The New York Times*, May 25, 2008, www.economist.com/node/11017644.

29. "Torts and Courts; Life, Liberty and the Pursuit of a Fair Judiciary," *The Economist*, April 10, 2008, www.economist.com/node/11017644.

30. Justice at Stake, "Negative Ads: Justice at Stake's 2008 Collection of Negative Campaign Ads," Justice at Stake video, 4:15, 2008, www.justiceatstake.org/video_etc/negative_ads.cfm.

31. Phillip Rawls, "Alabama Tops in Expensive Court Races," Associated Press, February 14, 2011, www.tuscaloosanews.com/article/20110214/news/110219807&tc=yahoo; Dana Beyerle, "State bar tells candidates to play nice," TimesDaily.com, October 15, 2008.

32. Charles Hall, ed., *The New Politics of Judicial Elections 2000-2009* (August 2010): 29.

33. Justice at Stake, "Judicial Elections 2010: Alabama Justice Tom

Parker compares 'Don't Ask, Don't Tell' Judge to Al Qaeda," Justice at Stake video, 1:02, 2010, www.justiceatstake.org/state/judicial _elections_2010/index.cfm.

34. Press-Register Editorial Board, "Expensive Campaigns for High Court Raise Questions," *Al.com*, February 15, 2011, http://blog .al.com/press-registercommentary/2011/02/editorial_expensive_ campaigns.html.

35. Ibid.

36. Patrick Marley, "Spending on High Court Race Topped $5 Million," *Journal Sentinel*, April 19, 2011.

37. Approximately $1.37, $911,000, and $836,000, respectively. Brennan Center for Justice, "Judicial Public Financing in Wisconsin —2011," April 5, 2011, www.brennancenter.org/content/resource/ judicial_public_financing_in_wisconsin_2011.

38. Kenneth P. Vogel, "Money Pours Into Wis. Court Race," *Politico*, April 4, 2011, http://dyn.politico.com/members/forums/thread .cfm?catid=1&subcatid=70&threadid=5288528.

39. Evan McMorris-Santoro, "Mother of All Negative Ads Dropped on WI Judicial Race," *TPMDC*, March 25, 2011, http://tpmdc .talkingpointsmemo.com/2011/03/welcome-to-the-wisconsin-judicial-race-home-of-the-negativiest-tv-ad-ever-video.php.

40. Annenberg Public Policy Center, "Americans overwhelmingly favor election of judges but disapprove of judicial campaign fundraising, fearing it affects fairness, according to a new Annenberg Public Policy Center study," press release, May 23, 2007, 1, 3.

41. Ibid.

42. Annenberg Public Policy Center, *2007 Annenberg Public Policy Center Judicial Survey Results*, October 17, 2007, 2.

43. Ibid., 3.

44. Justice at Stake, "Solid Bipartisan Majorities Believe Judges Influenced by Campaign Contributions: Independent Survey Caps Decade of Record-Shattering Judicial Elections," press release, September 8, 2010, www.commondreams.org/newswire /2010/09/08-6.

45. Quoted in Rebecca Love Kourlis, "America's Judicial Selection Wars," *Human Rights* 36 (Winter 2009): 7.

46. Ibid.

47. "Justice at Stake: State Judges Frequency Questionnaire," Justice at Stake, www.justiceatstake.org/media/cms/JASJudgesSurvey-Results_EA8838C0504A5.pdf (accessed March 14, 2011).

48. James Sample, "Justice for Sale," *Wall Street Journal*, March 22, 2008, http://online.wsj.com/article/SB120614225489456227.html ?mod=googlenews_wsj.

49. Justice at Stake and Committee for Economic Development, "Poll: West Virginia Voters Support Public Financing for Court Elections," 2010, www.justiceatstake.org/media/cms/West_Virginia_ Poll_Results_674E634FDB13F.pdf.

50. Richard Neely, *The Product Liability Mess: How Business Can Be Rescued from the Politics of State Courts* (New York: The Free Press, 1988) 4.

51. Eric Helland and Alexander Tabarrok, "The Effect of Electoral Institutions on Tort Awards," *American Law and Economics Review* 4 (2002): 350.

52. Gregory A. Huber and Sanford C. Gordon, "Accountability and Coercion: Is Justice Blind When It Runs for Office?," *American Journal of Political Science* 48 (April 2004): 247.

53. "Court System Reform a Pressing Problem," *Time*, February 21, 1955.

54. Interview with businessman, by Rebecca Love Kourlis (2010). The name of interviewee is withheld by mutual agreement.

55. Chief Justice Wallace B. Jefferson and Rebecca Love Kourlis, "An Analysis of Accountability in Judicial Selection: Recounting the Peril of Straight Party Voting," *The Advocate* 53 (Winter 2010): 8–9.

56. Ibid., 8.

57. Editorial, "Judging on the merits, not party labels," *Star-Telegram*, March 1, 2011.

58. "Methods of Judicial Selection—Selection of Judges," American Judicature Society, www.judicialselection.us/judicial_selection/ methods/selection_of_judges.cfm?state= (accessed April 5, 2011).

59. Daryl R. Yost, "A Lay Perspective on Merit Selection," memorandum to Rebecca Love Kourlis, April 21, 2011.

60. Ibid.

61. US Chamber Institute for Legal Reform, *Promoting 'Merit' in Merit Selection: A Best Practices Guide to Commission-Based Judicial Selection* (Washington, DC: US Chamber Institute for Legal Reform, October 2009): 3.

62. "2010 State Liability Systems Ranking Study," US Chamber Institute for Legal Reform, www.instituteforlegalreform.com/lawsuit-climate.html#/2010 (accessed March 14, 2011).

63. Steven M. Puiszis, ed., *Without Fear or Favor in 2011: A New Decade of Challenges to Judicial Independence and Accountability* (Chicago: DRI, 2011): 28.

64. National Center for State Courts, "Special Edition: Merit Selection," *Gavel to Gavel*, April 14, 2011.

65. Yost, "A Lay Perspective on Merit Selection."April 21, 2011.

66. American Bar Association and Harris Interactive, Poll on

Public Awareness of Judicial Selection, October 16, 2008, http://facethestate.com/sites/default/files/downloads/harrispoll_judicial selection.pdf.

67. Henry Kantor, interview by Dirk Olin, February 13, 2010.

68. Joel Stashenko and Noeleen G. Walder, "Recusal Is Step in Right Direction, Bar Leaders Say," *New York Law Journal*, February 15, 2011.

69. Ibid.

3. The Importance of Trials

1. James Surowiecki, *The Wisdom of the Crowds* (New York: Anchor Books, 2004).

2. Tim Cavanaugh, "Run Away, Jury!" *Reason*, November 2005, http://reason.com/archives/2005/11/01/run-away-jury.

3. Popular paraphrase of original writing, reprinted in J. Kendall Few, *Trial by Jury* (The American Jury Trial Foundation, 1993), 161.

4. Stephan Landsman, "The Civil Jury in America: Scenes from an Unappreciated History," *Hastings L. J.* 44 (1993): 579, 600.

5. *Annals of Congress*, 1st Cong., 1st sess., 453, (1789).

6. Thomas Jefferson, "Letter to the Abbé Arnoux, Paris, July 19, 1789," in Julian P. Boyd et al., ed., *The Papers of Thomas Jefferson* (Princeton, NJ: Princeton Univ. Press, 1950), 283.

7. National Center for State Courts, "Jury Managers' Toolbox: Best Practices for Jury Summons Enforcement" (2009).

8. Paula Hannaford-Agor, "Jury News: Tales of 'Tales' Juries," *The Court Manager* 23.2 (2008).

9. Andrew Villegas, "People Plucked Off Streets, Picked for Emergency Duty," *Greeley Tribune*, January 17, 2008.

10. Robert G. Boatright, "Why Citizens Don't Respond to Jury Summonses: And What Courts Can Do about It," *Judicature* 82.4 (1999): 162.

11. Ibid.

12. Harris Interactive, prepared for the American Bar Association, "Jury Service: Is Fulfilling Your Civic Duty a Trial?" (2004), 9.

13. Ibid.

14. Ibid., 11.

15. John Gastil, E. Pierre Deess, Philip J. Weiser, and Cindy Simmons, *The Jury and Democracy: How Jury Deliberation Promotes Civic Engagement and Political Participation* (Oxford: Oxford Univ. Press, 2010), 5.

16. Rebecca Love Kourlis and Gilbert A. Dickinson, "Why the Disappearance of Civil Jury Trials Is Not Acceptable," *Voir Dire* 17 (Fall/Winter 2010): 5.

17. Marc Galanter, "The Vanishing Trial: An Examination of Trials and Related Matters in Federal and State Courts," *Journal of Empirical Legal Studies* 1 (2004): 461.

18. See the Administrative Office of the United States Courts *Judicial Business of the United States Courts* annual publications from 2000 to 2010.

19. Marc Galanter and Angela Frozena, "'A grin without a cat': Civil Trials in the Federal Courts," 6 (May 1, 2010) (unpublished paper, prepared for presentation at the 2010 Civil Litigation Conference).

20. Ibid., 7.

21. Ibid.

22. Galanter, "The Vanishing Trial," 485.

23. Ibid., 489.

24. Galanter and Frozena, "'A grin without a cat,'" 1, 3.

25. Brian J. Ostrom, Shauna M. Strickland, and Paula L. Hannaford-Agor, "Examining Trial Trends in State Courts: 1976–2002," *Journal of Empirical Legal Studies* 1 (2004): 769.

26. Ibid., 768.

27. Administrative Office of the United States Courts, Judicial Business of the United States Courts 2010 (Washington, DC: US Government Printing Office, 2011): Table C-4A.

28. Administrative Office of the United States Courts, Judicial Business of the United States Courts 2000 (Washington, DC: US Government Printing Office, 2001): Table C-4A.

29. Henry Kantor, interview by Dirk Olin, February 13, 2010.

30. Joseph F. Anderson Jr., "Where Have You Gone, Spot Mozingo? A Trial Judge's Lament Over the Demise of the Civil Jury Trial," *Federal Courts Law Review* 4 (2010): 102.

31. Ibid.

32. Ming Chin, interview by Dirk Olin, January 21, 2011.

33. Ibid.

34. Shari Seidman Diamond, "Beyond Fantasy and Nightmare: A Portrait of the Jury," *Buffalo Law Review* 54 (2006): 730.

35. Harry Kalven Jr. and Hans Zeisel, *The American Jury* (Boston: Little, Brown and Co., 1966), 63–64.

36. Ibid., 64.

37. Kevin M. Clermont and Theodore Eisenberg, "Litigation Realities," *Cornell Law Review* 88 (November 2002): 145.

38. Ibid., 144.

39. Ibid., 145.

40. Larry Heuer and Steven Penrod, "Trial Complexity: A Field Investigation of Its Meaning and Its Effects," *Law and Human Behavior* 18 (1994): 46, 48.

41. Daniel J. Shapiro, "Punitive Damages in Louisiana: A Year of Controversy," *Louisiana Bar Journal* 43(1995): 253, note 1.
42. Diamond, "Beyond Fantasy and Nightmare," 747–48.
43. Institute for the Advancement of the American Legal System, *Civil Case Processing in the Federal District Courts: A 21st Century Analysis* (Denver: IAALS, 2009), 49–50.
44. Joe S. Cecil, Rebecca N. Eyre, Dean Miletich, and David Rindskopf, "A Quarter-Century of Summary Judgment Practice in Six Federal District Courts," *Journal of Empirical Legal Studies* 4 (December 2007): 882.
45. Ibid., 883.
46. IAALS, *Civil Case Processing*, 51.
47. Emery G. Lee III and Thomas E. Willging, *Litigation Costs in Civil Cases: Multivariate Analysis* 6, 8 (Washington, DC: Federal Judicial Center, March 2010).
48. Thomas J. Stipanowich, "ADR and the 'Vanishing Trial': The Growth and Impact of 'Alternative Dispute Resolution,'" *Journal of Empirical Legal Studies* 1 (November 2004): 911.
49. Janice Davidson, interview by Dirk Olin, January 20, 2011.
50. Gina Passarella, "Litigators Losing Love of Arbitration Argue for Trials," *Law.com*, September 1, 2010, www.law.com/jsp/article.jsp?id=1202471400934&slreturn=1&hbxlogin=1.
51. Douglas Shontz, Fred Kipperman, and Vanessa Soma, *Business-to-Business Arbitration in the United States: Perceptions of Corporate Counsel* (Santa Monica: Rand Corporation, 2011), x.
52. Passarella, "Litigators Losing Love of Arbitration."
53. Sheri Qualters, "Two Federal Judges Offer Differing Takes on Declining Trial Numbers," *National Law Journal* (September 20, 2010). A recording of the panel can be accessed at www.fedbar.org/Chapters/Massachusetts-Chapter/Recent-Events.aspx.
54. Jack Zouhary, interview by Dirk Olin, January 17, 2011.
55. Ibid.
56. Qualters, "Two Federal Judges Offer Differing Takes."
57. Ibid.
58. Ibid. A fuller discussion of proposals to reform court management and measurement can be found in chapters 7 and 8.
59. Judith Resnik, "Courts: In and Out of Sight, Site, and Cite: The Norman Shachoy Lecture," *Villanova Law Review* 53 (2008): 795.
60. Randy Kennedy, "That Lady With the Scales Poses for Her Portraits," *The New York Times*, December 15, 2010.
61. Dennis M. Sweeney, "Worlds Collide: The Digital Native Enters the Jury Box," *Reynolds Courts & Media Law Journal* 1(2011): 128.
62. Ibid., 129.

63. David J. Beck, "The Consequences of the Vanishing Trial: Does Anyone Really Care?" *Houston Law Review*, 29 (2010): 40.

64. Ibid.

65. John P. Foley, ed., *The Jefferson Cyclopedia: A Comprehensive Collection of the Views of Thomas Jefferson* (New York: Funk & Wagnalls Co., 1900), 450.

66. Beck, "The Consequences of the Vanishing Trial," 40.

4. Funding Justice and Fostering Innovation

1. Chief Justice John Roberts, "2006 Year-End Report on the Federal Judiciary" (January 1, 2007), 6, www.supremecourt.gov/public info/year-end/2006year-endreport.pdf.

2. American Bar Association, "Recommendations on Judicial Cost-of-Living Adjustments" (February 8–9, 2010), 3.

3. Ibid.

4. Roberts, "2006 Year-End Report," 3.

5. Steven M. Puiszis, ed., *Without Fear or Favor in 2011: A New Decade of Challenges to Judicial Independence and Accountability* (Chicago: DRI, 2011) 77.

6. Roberts, "2006 Year-End Report," 6.

7. ABA, "Recommendations," 3.

8. Puiszis, *Without Fear or Favor*, 70.

9. Ibid.

10. "Judicial Vacancies: Judicial Emergencies," United States Courts, www.uscourts.gov/JudgesAndJudgeships/JudicialVacancies/JudicialEmergencies.aspx (accessed April 12, 2011).

11. Chief Justice John Roberts, "2010 Year-End Report on the Federal Judiciary," (December 31, 2010), 5, www.supremecourt.gov/public info/year-end/2010year-endreport.pdf.

12. "State Activities Map: Percent of Change for Fiscal Year 2010," National Center for State Courts, www.ncsc.org/information-and-resources/budget-resource-center/states-activities-map.aspx (accessed March 14, 2011).

13. National Center for State Courts, Court Statistics Project, *Examining the Work of State Courts: An Analysis of 2008 State Court Caseloads* (Williamsburg, VA: National Center for State Courts, 2010), 19.

14. "State Activities Map: Specific Cost-Saving Measures," National Center for State Courts, www.ncsc.org/information-and-resources/budget-resource-center/states-activities-map.aspx (accessed March 14, 2011).

15. Jeff German, "Justice Court Clerk's Office to Close for a Week to Deal with Backlog of Cases," *Las Vegas Review-Journal*, December 20, 2010, www.lvrj.com/news/justice-court-clerk-s-office-to-

close-for-a-week-to-deal-with-backlog-of-cases-112220474.html.

16. Dana Wilson, "Budget Pinch in Morrow County: Paperless court is motionless," *Columbus Dispatch*, March 14, 2009, www .dispatch.com/live/content/local_news/stories/2009/03/14/morrow ct.ART_ART_03-14-09_A1_4HD7RR4.html.

17. Sheri Qualters, "New Hampshire Lawyers Sue State Over Court Budget Cuts and Delays," *National Law Journal*, September 29, 2010, www.law.com/jsp/article.jsp?id=1202472670712&New_ Hampshire_Lawyers_Sue_State_Over_Budget_Cuts_and_ Delays&slreturn=1&hbxlogin=1.

18. Daniel J. Hall and Thomas Clarke, "Delivering Judicial Services in Hard Times," in *Future Trends in State Courts 2008*, Carol R. Flango, Amy M. McDowell, Charles F. Campbell, and Neal B. Kauder, eds. (Williamsburg, VA: National Center for State Courts, 2008), 4.

19. Maria Dakolias, "Court Performance around the World: A Comparative Perspective" (discussion paper, World Bank Technical Paper No. 430, World Bank, Washington, DC, July 1999), 1–2.

20. The Washington Economics Group, Inc., "The Economic Impact on the Georgia Economy of Delays in Georgia's State Courts Due to Recent Reductions in Funding for the Judicial System," 3 (rev. Jan. 24, 2011).

21. Ibid., 11.

22. Stephen N. Zack, "Solve the crisis in state courts," AJC.com, February 8, 2011, www.ajc.com/opinion/solve-the-crisis-in-831821 .html.

23. National Center for State Courts, "ABA Task Force Hears Testimony on 'crossroad period in civil justice,'" news release, February 9, 2011, www.ncsc.org/Newsroom/ABA-hearing.aspx.

24. Brian Ostrom and Roger Hanson, "Achieving High Performance: A Framework for Courts" (working paper 85, National Center for State Courts, Research Division, 2010), 85, www.ncsconline.org/ wikis/ctf/images/7/74/Achieving_High_Performance_Courts_ Framework_-_April_2010.pdf.

25. Thomas M. Clarke, "Reengineering: The Importance of Establishing Principles," in *Future Trends in State Courts 2010*, Carol R. Flango, Amy M. McDowell, Charles F. Campbell, and Neal B. Kauder eds. (Williamsburg, VA: National Center for State Courts, 2010), 30.

26. Hon. John T. Broderick Jr. and Daniel J. Hall, "What Is Reengineering and Why Is It Necessary?," in *Future Trends in State Courts 2010*, Amy M. McDowell, Charles F. Campbell, and Neal B. Kauder eds. (Williamsburg, VA: National Center for State Courts, 2010), 25.

27. Judge Kevin S. Burke, "It Is All About the People Who Work in the Courthouse," in *Future Trends in State Courts 2011* Amy M. McDowell, Charles F. Campbell, and Neal B. Kauder eds.(Williamsburg, VA: National Center for State Courts, forthcoming 2011).

28. Frank Broccolina and Richard Zorza, "En$uring Access to Ju$tice in Tough Economic Times," *Judicature* 92 (November-December 2008): 125.

29. Henry Kantor, interview by Dirk Olin, February 13, 2010.

30. Lael Montgomery, interview by Dirk Olin, January 12, 2011.

31. Ibid.

32. Marcus Reinkensmeyer, interview by Dirk Olin, January 13, 2011.

33. Ibid.

34. Ibid.

35. Ibid.

36. Melinda Taylor, interview by Dirk Olin, January 10, 2011.

37. Sue Dosal, interview by Dirk Olin, February 1, 2011.

38. Ibid.

39. Ibid.

40. Ostrom and Hanson, "Achieving High Performance," ii.

5. Discovery: The Deluge

1. John W. Reed, "Light-Hearted Thoughts About Discovery Reform," *Review of Litigation* 3 (1982–1983): 220–221.

2. Ibid., 221.

3. Ibid.

4. Emery G. Lee III and Thomas E. Willging, *Litigation Costs in Civil Cases: Multivariate Analysis* (Washington, DC: Federal Judicial Center, March 2010), 5–7.

5. Jill Griset, interview by Dirk Olin, January 29, 2011.

6. Ibid.

7. Ibid.

8. Institute for the Advancement of the American Legal System, *Electronic Discovery: A View from the Front Lines* (Denver: IAALS, 2008), 5.

9. Ibid.

10. Ibid., citing Alan Cohen, "Data, Data Everywhere," *Corporate Counsel*, July 2007, 78.

11. Cohen, "Data, Data Everywhere," 78.

12. IAALS, *Electronic Discovery*, 7.

13. IAALS, *Civil Litigation Survey of Chief Legal Officers and General Counsel Belonging to the Association of Corporate Council* (Denver: IAALS, 2010), 16.

14. Ibid.

15. Ibid., 37.
16. Gregory P. Joseph, "Electronic Discovery and Other Problems" (2009). Paper submitted to the 2010 Conference on Civil Litigation, available at http://civilconference.uscourts.gov.
17. IAALS, *Electronic Discovery*, 20.
18. Ibid., 5.
19. Ibid.
20. James N. Dertouzos, Nicholas M. Pace, and Robert H. Anderson, "The Legal and Economic Implications of Electronic Discovery: Options for Future Research (Santa Monica, CA: Rand Corporation, 2008), 3.
21. IAALS, *Electronic Discovery*, 16.
22. Ibid., 5.
23. Ibid.
24. Ming Chin, interview by Dirk Olin, January 21, 2011.
25. Ibid.
26. IAALS, *Electronic Discovery*, 9.
27. Ibid.
28. Ibid., 18.
29. Ibid., 11.
30. IAALS, *Civil Litigation Survey*, 30.
31. Ibid.
32. American College of Trial Lawyers and Institute for the Advancement of the American Legal System, "Final Report on the Joint Project of the American College of Trial Lawyers Task Force on Discovery and the Institute for the Advancement of the American Legal System," 2.
33. IAALS, *Electronic Discovery*, 18.
34. *Zubulake v. UBS Warburg, LLC*, 217 F.R.D. 309 (S.D.N.Y. 2003) (Zubulake I), 230 F.R.D. 290 (S.D.N.Y. 2003) (Zubulake II), 216 F.R.D. 280 (S.D.N.Y. 2003) (Zubulake III), 220 F.R.D. 212 (S.D.N.Y. 2003) (Zubulake IV), 229 F.R.D. 422 (S.D.N.Y. 2004) (Zubulake V), 382 F.Supp.2d 536 (S.D.N.Y. 2005) (Zubulake VI).
35. See *Federal Rules of Civil Procedure* 26(b)(2)(B) and 26(f)(3)C).
36. *Pension Committee of the University of Montreal Pension Plan v. Banc of America Securities, LLC*, 685 F. Supp. 2d 456, 461–62 (S.D.N.Y. Jan. 15, 2010).

6. The Conestoga Wagon on the Information Highway

1. Jay Tidmarsh, "Pound's Century and Ours," *Notre Dame L. Rev.* 81 (2006): 513, 518.
2. Stephen C. Yeazell, "Judging Rules, Ruling Judges," *Law and Contemporary Problems* 61 (1998): 233.

3. Robert G. Bone, "The Process of Making Process: Court Rule-making, Democratic Legitimacy, and Procedural Efficacy," *Georgetown Law Journal* 87(1999): 898.

4. *Hickman v. Taylor*, 329 U.S. 495, 507 (1947).

5. Mark Hansen, "Rethinking the Rules: Begin with the End in Mind" (presentation, 10th Circuit Bench and Bar Conference, Colorado Springs, Colorado, August 26, 2010).

6. "Antitrust: The Monster Case," *Time*, June 2, 1975, www.time.com/time/magazine/article/0,9171,913094,00.html.

7. Steven Flanders, *Case Management and Court Management in United States District Courts* (Washington, DC: Federal Judicial Center, 1977); Paul R. Connolly, Edith A. Holleman, and Michael J. Kuhlman, *Judicial Controls and the Civil Litigative Process: Discovery* (Washington, DC: Federal Judicial Center, 1978).

8. Harris Interactive, "Public Trust of Civil Justice" (June 20, 2005), 8, 10.

9. Corina Gerety, *Excess and Access: Consensus on the American Civil Justice Landscape* (Denver: Institute for the Advancement of the American Legal System, 2011), 9.

10. Institute for the Advancement of the American Legal System, *Civil Litigation Survey of Chief Legal Officers and General Counsel Belonging to the Association of Corporate Counsel* (2010), 18.

11. Gerety, *Excess and Access*, 9.

12. Kirsten Barrett, Rhoda Cohen, and John Hall, *ACTL Civil Litigation Survey: Final Report* (Princeton, NJ: Mathematica Policy Research, Inc., 2008), 74; American Bar Association Section of Litigation, *ABA Section of Litigation Member Survey on Civil Practice: Detailed Report* (Chicago: American Bar Association, 2009), 6, 172; Rebecca M. Hamburg and Matthew C. Koski, National Employment Lawyers Association, *Summary of Results of Federal Judicial Center Survey of NELA Members, Fall 2009* (March 26, 2010): 45.

13. Gerety, *Excess and Access*, 9.

14. Ibid., 11.

15. "Federal Court Management Statistics 2010: All District Courts," United States Courts, www.uscourts.gov/viewer.aspx?doc=/cgi-bin/cmsd2010Sep.pl (accessed March 14, 2011).

16. IAALS, *Civil Case Processing in the Federal District Courts: A 21st Century Analysis* (Denver: IAALS, 2009), 37.

17. IAALS, *Excess and Access*, 9; IAALS, *Civil Litigation Survey*, 20.

18. Emery G. Lee III and Thomas E. Willging, *Litigation Costs in Civil Cases: Multivariate Analysis* (Washington, DC: Federal Judicial Center, March 2010), 5, 7.

19. Gerety, *Excess and Access*, 11.

20. Ibid.

21. IAALS, *Civil Case Processing*, 28. The study does not explicitly account for vacant judge months in the Eastern District of Virginia—the only court in the study with recorded judicial vacancies during the 2005–2006 period.

22. Judicial Council of California Task Force on Self-Represented Litigants, *Statewide Action Plan for Self-Represented Litigants* (California: Judicial Council of California, 2004), 11.

23. New Hampshire Supreme Court Task Force on Self-Representation, *Challenge to Justice: A Report on Self-Represented Litigants in New Hampshire Courts* (Concord: State of New Hampshire Judicial Branch, 2004), 2.

24. American Bar Association Coalition for Justice, *Report on the Survey of Judges on the Impact of the Economic Downturn on Representation in the Courts* (preliminary report, Coalition for Justice, American Bar Association, 2010), 3.

25. Ibid., 4.

26. Chief Justice John T. Broderick Jr. (speech given at the National Access to Justice Conference Minneapolis, Minnesota, May 9, 2008). Reprinted in ABA Division for Legal Services, Dialogue 12 (Summer 2008): 29.

27. Ibid.

28. Ibid.

29. Association of Corporate Counsel, "ACC Value Challenge—About," www.acc.com/valuechallenge/about/index.cfm (accessed April 25, 2011).

30. Ibid.

31. Paul W. Grimm and Elizabeth J. Cabraser, "The State of Discovery Practice in Civil Cases: Must the Rules be Changed to Reduce Costs and Burdens, or can Significant Improvements be Achieved within the Existing Rules?" (conference presentation, 2010 Conference on Civil Litigation, May 10–11, 2010), 4.

32. Ibid., 11.

33. Lee H. Rosenthal, "From Rules of Procedure to How Lawyers Litigate: 'Twixt the Cup and the Lip,'" *University of Denver Law Review* 87 (2010): 230.

34. Ibid., 231.

35. Broderick (speech, May 9, 2008), 31.

7. Changing the Process: It Is Time

1. Chief Justice Barton R. Voigt, "2010 State of the Judiciary" (speech, Joint Session of the Wyoming State Legislature, Cheyenne,

Wyoming, February 8, 2010), 19–20.

2. Ibid., 19–20.

3. Mark David Agrast, Juan Carlos Botero, and Alejandro Ponce, World Justice Project, *Rule of Law Index 2010* (Washington, DC: World Justice Project, 2010): 18

4. Ibid., 93.

5. After Japan, France, Canada, Spain, Australia, South Korea, Austria, Netherlands, Sweden, and Singapore—from lowest to highest. Ibid., 95. In the 2011 report, cited at endnote 6, the World Justice Project only examined seventy countries, with plans to expand the pool to one hundred countries by 2012. Ibid., 2.

6. Mark David Agrast, Juan Carlos Botero, and Alejandro Ponce, World Justice Project, *Rule of Law Index 2011* (Washington, DC: World Justice Project, 2011): 23.

7. Institute for the Advancement of the American Legal System, *A Summary of Comparative Approaches to Civil Procedure* (Denver: IAALS, 2009), 7.

8. Ibid., 6.

9. Ibid.

10. IAALS, *Survey of the Arizona Bench and Bar on the Arizona Rules of Civil Procedure* (Denver: IAALS, 2010), 12.

11. Ibid., 15.

12. Ibid., 14.

13. IAALS, *Survey of the Oregon Bench and Bar on the Oregon Rules of Civil Procedure* (Denver: IAALS, 2010), 12–14.

14. IAALS, *2010 Annual Report: Advancing Solutions for Tomorrow's Legal System* (2011), 6.

15. Jack Zouhary, interview by Dirk Olin, January 17, 2011.

16. *Physicians Choice of Arizona, Inc. v. Miller*, Rulings on Pending Motions, CV 2003-020242 (July 21, 2006).

17. Carl Tobias, "Complex Litigation at the Millennium: A Modest Reform for Federal Procedural Rulemaking," *Law and Contemporary Problems* 64 (2001): 286.

8. Divorce Court

1. "Cuyahoga County Domestic Relations Court Is Slow, Costly," *Cleveland Plain Dealer*, August 18, 2008, http://blog.cleveland .com/metro/2008/08/county_court_is_slow_costly.html.

2. Ibid.

3. Ibid.

4. Anonymous individual, informal conversation with Rebecca Love Kourlis.

5. National Center for Health Statistics, "Births, Marriages,

Divorces, and Deaths: Provisional Data for November 2009," *National Vital Statistics Reports* 58, no. 23 (July 29, 2010). This figure excludes divorce data for California, Georgia, Hawaii, Indiana, Louisiana, and Minnesota.

6. Betsey Stevenson and Justin Wolfers, "Divorced From Reality," *The New York Times*, September 29, 2007.

7. See Betsey Stevenson and Justin Wolfers, "Marriage and Divorce: Changes and their Driving Forces," *Journal of Economic Perspectives* 21 (Spring 2007): 40.

8. Paul R. Amato, "The Consequences of Divorce for Adults and Children," *Journal of Marriage and the Family* 62, no. 4 (2000): 126.

9. "Key Statistics from the National Survey of Family Growth: Cohabitation with the opposite sex," Centers for Disease Control and Prevention, www.cdc.gov/nchs/nsfg/abc_list_c.htm# chabitation (accessed March 14, 2011).

10. Gladys M. Martinez, Anjani Chandra, Joyce C. Abma, Jo Jones, and William D. Mosher, *Fertility, Contraception, and Fatherhood: Data on Men and Women from Cycle 6 (2002) of the National Survey of Family Growth* (Washington, DC: National Center for Health Statistics, 2006), 6.

11. Pew Research Center, "The Decline of Marriage and Rise of New Families," *Social and Demographic Trends Report*, November 18, 2010, iii.

12. Bruce Peterson, interview by Dirk Olin, October 5, 2010.

13. National Center for State Courts, *Examining the Work of State Courts: An Analysis of 2008 State Court Caseloads* (Williamsburg, VA: National Center for State Courts, 2010), 19.

14. Ibid., 38.

15. Justice Leah Ward Sears, ret., "Nation's Divorce Culture Now Overburdening Our Court Systems," *Unified Family Court Connection* (Winter 2011): 1.

16. Ibid.

17. Ibid.

18. Bruce Peterson, interview by Dirk Olin, October 5, 2010.

19. Melinda S. Forthoffer, Howard J. Markman, Martha Cox, Scott Stanley, and Ronald C. Kessler, "Associations between Marital Distress and Work Loss in a National Sample," *Journal of Marriage and Family* 58, no. 3 (1996).

20. Howard J. Markmann, Jack Myrick, and Marcie A. Pregulman, "Marriage Education in the Workplace," *Journal of Employee Assistance* 36 (July 2006): 14.

21. Ibid.

22. Forthoffer et al., "Associations between Marital Stress," 602.

23. David G. Schramm, "Individual and Social Costs of Divorce in Utah," *Journal of Family and Economic Issues* 133, no. 27 (April 2006): 146; David G. Schramm, "Estimated Costs of Divorce," on file with IAALS.

24. Barbara A. Babb, "Reevaluating Where We Stand: A Comprehensive Survey of America's Family Justice Systems," *Family Court Review* 46 (April 2008): 230.

25. Judicial Council of California Task Force on Self-Represented Litigants, "Statewide Action Plan for Self-Represented Litigants" (San Francisco: Judicial Council of California, 2004), 11.

26. Committee on Resources for Self-Represented Parties, *Strategic Planning Initiative: Report to the Utah Judicial Council* (Salt Lake City: Committee on Resources for Self-Represented Parties, July 25, 2006), 5.

27. Barbara Babb, interview by Dirk Olin, October 4, 2010.

28. Ibid.

29. Colorado Rule of Civil Procedure 16.2 (2011).

30. Florida State Courts Office of Court Improvement/Family Courts Main Page, www.flcourts.org/gen_public/family/familycourts.shtml.

31. State of Connecticut Judicial Branch—Court Support Services Division, History of Court Support Services Division, www.jud.ct .gov/CSSD/history.htm.

32. *The Family Court Act of 2001*, §11-908A(b), 115 Stat. 2100 (2002).

33. California Family Code Sec. 3161 (2011).

34. The Subordinate Courts of Singapore, Family Relations Chambers, http://app.subcourts.gov.sg/Data/Files/File/Family/Brochure /BrochureFC_FRC.pdf.

35. Australian National Audit Office, Department of Families, Housing, Community Services and Indigenous Affairs, *Implementation of the Family Relationship Centres Initiative* (Australia: Attorney-General's Department, 2010), 80.

36. See British Columbia, Ministry of Attorney General, Family Justice Centres, available for download at www.ag.gov.bc.ca/ family-justice.

37. Sterling T. Shumway, Richard S. Wampler, Charette Dersch, and Rudy Arredondo, "A Place for Marriage and Family Services in Employee Assistance Programs (EAPs): A Survey of EAP Client Problems and Needs," *Journal of Marital and Family Therapy* 30 (January 2004): 72.

38. Ellen Galinsky et al., *2008 National Study of Employers* (New York: Families and Work Institute, 2008): 6.

39. Barbara Babb, interview by Dirk Olin, October 4, 2010.

40. Ibid.

9. Insiders Speak

1. The interviews in this chapter were conducted by Dirk Olin from 2010 to 2011.

Primer: Courts and Lawsuits 101

1. Hamilton Abert Long, *The American Ideal of 1776: The Twelve Basic American Principles* (Philadelphia, PA: Your Heritage Books, 1976).

2. United States Courts, Federal Judicial Center Caseload Statistics, Caseload Statistics 2010, Tables B, C, D (12-month period ending March 31, 2011), www.uscourts.gov/Statistics/FederalJudicial CaseloadStatistics/FederalJudicialCaseloadStatistics2010.aspx.

3. National Center for State Courts, *Examining the Work of State Courts: An Analysis of 2008 State Court Caseloads* (Williamsburg, VA: National Center for State Courts, 2010), 25.

Glossary

alternative dispute resolution (ADR). A term that can cover a variety of mechanisms undertaken out of court, or as part of a court's case management tools, including arbitration, mediation, and early-neutral-evaluation. ADR may be undertaken by court-employed or privately funded individuals.

appellate court. A court whose function is to review what happened in the trial court and determine whether the judge made errors that require a different outcome or repeating the process. Appellate courts do not conduct trials or hear evidence. If the appellate court finds errors, sometimes the court merely reverses the lower court decision and the case ends. Sometimes, the court sends the case back to the trial court (called remand) for further proceedings, conducted according to requirements spelled out by the appellate court. Proceedings in these courts include the parties' filing of written arguments (briefs), sometimes oral presentations by the parties, and then a written opinion by the panel of the court assigned to decide the case.

binding arbitration. The process by which the parties choose and pay one or more arbitrators to decide the case. Those decision makers then set the schedule for the case, handle the discovery disputes, and hear the "trial." At an arbitration hearing, both sides present their evidence and then the arbitrator(s) makes a decision. That decision is not appealable except in extraordinary circumstances.

case management. The process whereby judges actively manage events throughout the life of a case. (The alternative is for the judge to sit passively, taking action only when the parties request that she or he do something.)

civil case. A case involving a dispute that does not involve the alleged commission of a crime. Generally, but not always, money is in dispute. In civil cases, the plaintiff (an individual or group of individuals) or entity such as a business, partnership, governmental agency, etc., files a complaint against the defendant.

complaint. The document filed by the party bringing the lawsuit (the plaintiff), which commences a civil case.

contested judicial election. An election in which multiple candidates may seek the same judicial position. Voters cast ballots for judicial candidates as they do for candidates for other public offices.

criminal case. A case brought by the government (the prosecution is listed as the "United States," the "State" or "People") against an individual (defendant) alleging that the defendant committed a crime. Punishment can include the loss of liberty.

discovery. The pretrial process by which parties to a lawsuit request information from each other. That information can come in the form of formal questions, documents, or oral examination under oath.

electronic discovery (e-discovery). The discovery of electronically stored information.

electronically stored information (ESI). All information that is stored on an electronic medium, including audio and video files, e-mail messages, instant messages, voice mails, text messages, webpages, call logs, word processing documents, databases, digital photos, spreadsheets and accounting software, and specialized engineering software, as well as backup and archived copies of such information.

family case. A case involving family issues, such as estate matters (probate), divorce (dissolution of marriage), child support or custody (allocation of parental rights and responsibilities). These are civil cases, but are discussed separately for the purposes of this book, as they raise specific issues and challenges.

federal court system. The system comprising federal district and bankruptcy courts (trial courts), courts of appeals (appellate courts), and the US Supreme Court. The federal system also includes a few highly specialized trial and appellate courts. Other courts on the federal level are located in the executive branch and are not part of the federal judicial system.

federal courts of appeals. The system of intermediate appellate courts in the federal court system, each one functioning within a circuit, a geographic division that also includes district and bankruptcy courts. There are twelve regional circuits and the federal circuit (whose court of appeals has a national jurisdiction to hear certain types of cases). Circuits include clusters of states or US territories. The Ninth Circuit, for example, covers Alaska, Arizona, California, Idaho, Montana, Nevada, Oregon, Washington, Guam, the Northern Mariana Islands, and Hawaii. The Second Circuit covers Connecticut, New York, and Vermont.

federal district court. The principal trial court in the federal system. Federal district courts handle both civil and criminal (but almost never family) matters. There is one or more district courts in each state. These courts have jurisdiction over three general types of civil cases—cases involving a federal law or the US Constitution (called federal question jurisdiction, including suits by prisoners challenging the constitutionality of their convictions in state or federal courts), cases in which a citizen of one state sues a citizen of another state based on state, not federal law, for at least $75,000 (called diversity jurisdiction), and—in limited circumstances—cases involving state claims that are mixed with federal claims (called ancillary jurisdiction). Federal courts also handle actions challenging the constitutionality of the apportionment of congressional districts.

Federal Rules of Civil Procedure (Federal Rules). The set of rules and procedures governing all civil cases in federal courts. Additionally, many states have implemented the Federal Rules in whole or in part.

Federal Rules of Criminal Procedure. The set of rules and procedures governing all criminal cases in federal courts.

gubernatorial appointment. The process by which a judge is appointed by a state governor (without input from a judicial nominating commission). Depending on the state, the appointment may require confirmation by the legislature or an executive council.

interrogatories. A tool of discovery consisting of questions from one party to another party in the lawsuit. The questions contained in the interrogatories should be questions that allow the other side to understand exactly what the nature of the claims and defenses might be.

judicial performance evaluation (JPE). Programs that are an approach to promoting judicial accountability without unnecessarily restricting judicial independence. State judicial performance commissions evaluate state judges on neutral criteria related to the process of judging, rather than on specific case outcomes. These programs can be shaped in many different ways to meet the specific needs of a state's judiciary and citizenry.

legislative appointment/election. The process by which state judges are appointed or elected by legislative vote only.

mediation. The kinder, gentler form of ADR. In mediation, the parties work with a settlement judge or an actual trained mediator to try to reach agreement about the outcome of the case. When the mediation is handled by a judge (usually not the judge who will hear the case in court), it is sometimes called a settlement conference and is an opportunity for a judge to tell the parties and counsel how that judge views the facts and the law so that they have a basis upon which to decide whether to settle. Other kinds of mediation work differently, but all seek to bring the parties themselves to agreement.

merit selection. The process by which judicial applicants to be state judges are evaluated by a nominating commission, which then sends the names of the candidates it considers best qualified to the governor. The governor appoints one of the nominees submitted by the commission. (Some observers object to the term *merit selection*, because it may imply that judges selected through other methods lack merit.)

metadata. Information about electronically stored files that is contained within the file itself or in a linked database. It typically contains information such as the file's author, all recipients, the dates on which the file was created, modified, read, accessed by recipients, or printed, and all changes that have been made to the file.

minute order. An abbreviated court order entered by the judge or court clerk.

nonpartisan judicial election. An election in which a judicial candidate's party affiliation, if any, is not designated on the ballot.

partisan judicial election. An election in which candidates run for a judicial position with the official endorsement of a political party. The candidate's party affiliation is listed on the ballot.

petition for writ of certiorari. The US Supreme Court, along with many state supreme courts, has the discretion to hear or decline to hear cases. A petition for writ of certiorari (or cert petition) is a request for the court to take a case filed by a party seeking to overturn a lower court's decision.

requests for admission. A tool of discovery in which one party asks an opposing party to admit a fact or contention at issue in the dispute.

summary judgment. Juries are supposed to decide facts and judges law. However, a judge can resolve a case, or part of a case, summarily, without hearing or trial, if he or she determines that there are no undisputed issues of fact on point and judgment is warranted as a matter of law.

tort. A type of civil action involving a breach of duty owed to another but does not include breach of a contract. Examples of tort actions include bodily injury or property damage, false imprisonment, and unfair business practices.

US Supreme Court. The highest court in the nation. In only very limited instances can a case be filed with the US Supreme Court first (original jurisdiction)—cases involving controversies between two states or a state and the Unites States, or in certain actions involving foreign nationals. More commonly, a party seeks to appeal the decision of a lower court through a petition for writ of certiorari, which the Court has discretion to approve or deny.

voir dire. The process whereby potential jurors are questioned by the judge and/or parties' attorneys to determine the suitability of potential jurors for a particular case.

Index

Rebecca Love Kourlis is the executive director of the Institute for the Advancement of the American Legal System at the University of Denver. She served for eleven years as a justice of the Colorado Supreme Court and eight years as a trial court judge in north-western Colorado. She holds undergraduate and law degrees from Stanford University and is the recipient of numerous awards, including the ABA Yegge Award for Outstanding Contribution in the Field of Judicial Administration in 2009; Regis University Civis Princeps Award in 2008; and the Colorado Judicial Institute's 2006 Judicial Independence Award. She is married to Tom Kourlis, a sheep and cattle rancher and former commissioner of agriculture in Colorado. Tom and Becky were named Citizens of the West in 2010. They have three children.

Dirk Olin is the editor and publisher of *Corporate Responsibility Magazine*. Formerly the director of the Institute for Judicial Studies and the national editor of *The American Lawyer* magazine, Olin has written for *The New York Times* op-ed pages and *The New York Times Magazine*, *The New Republic*, and *Slate*, among others. He is a fellow with the Institute for the Advancement of the American Legal System, a former visiting scholar at UC Berkeley's Institute of Governmental Studies, and a recipient of the National Education Writer's award. He has also been featured frequently on television and radio broadcasts. Currently board president of the International Debate Education Association, Olin has a master's degree from Northwestern Journalism School and a bachelor's degree from Dartmouth College. He lives in Maplewood, New Jersey, with his wife and their two daughters.

UNIVERSITY OF DENVER | INSTITUTE *for the* ADVANCEMENT *of the* AMERICAN LEGAL SYSTEM

The Institute for the Advancement of the American Legal System (IAALS) is a national, nonpartisan 'think-do' tank located at the University of Denver, with a mission of participating constructively in achieving a transparent, fair, and cost-effective legal system that is accountable to and trusted by those whom it serves. IAALS conducts empirical and legal research and works with teams of judges, lawyers, and other stakeholders to develop innovative and practical solutions to the problems plaguing the system. IAALS has four initiative areas: judicial selection and performance evaluation; the Rule 1 initiative, dealing with rules reform and caseflow management; and domestic relations reform and Educating Tomorrow's Lawyers, an initiative that seeks to develop better lawyers through innovative legal education.

Institute for the Advancement of the American Legal System
University of Denver
2060 South Gaylord Way
Denver, CO 80210
(P) 303-871-6600
(F) 303-871-6610
http://legalinstitute.du.edu